Children's Sermons
That Connect

Children's Sermons That Connect

70 Evangelistic and Spiritual Growth Messages Including Special Occasions

By
Frank R. Shivers

LIGHTNING SOURCE
1246 Heil Quaker Blvd.
La Vergne, TN

Unless otherwise noted, Scripture quotations are from
The Holy Bible *King James Version*

Library of Congress Cataloging-in-Publication Data

Shivers, Frank R., 1949–
Children's Sermons That Connect / Frank Shivers
ISBN
978-1-878127-18-1
Library of Congress Control Number:
2013902774
Cover design by
Tim King of Click Graphics, Inc.

For Information:
Frank Shivers Evangelistic Association
P. O. Box 9991
Columbia, South Carolina 29290
www.frankshivers.com

To

My grandchildren, Madison Clark and Jude Edward
McLawhorn

But Jesus said, "Let the children come to me. Don't stop them!
For the Kingdom of Heaven belongs to those who are like
these children."—Matthew 19:14 NLT

Contents

In *Come Ye Children,* C. H. Spurgeon stated, "As soon as a child is capable of being lost, it is capable of being saved. As soon as a child can sin, that child can, if God's grace assist it, believe and receive the Word of God....Believe that children can be saved just as much as yourselves. I do most firmly believe in the salvation of children. When you see the young heart brought to the Savior, do not stand by and speak harshly, mistrusting everything."[1]

What to tell a child? Spurgeon suggests, "Tell him he must be born again. Don't bolster him up with the fancy of his own innocence, but show him his sin. Mention the childish sins to which he is prone, and pray the Holy Spirit to work conviction in his heart and conscience. Deal with the young in much the same way as you would with the old. Be thorough and honest with them. These boys and girls need pardon through the precious blood as surely as any of us. Do not hesitate to tell the child his ruin; he will not else desire the remedy. Tell him also of the punishment of sin, and warn him of its terror. Be tender, but be true. Do not hide from the youthful sinner the truth, however terrible it may be. Now that he has come to years of responsibility, if he believes not in Christ, it will go ill with him at the last great day. Set before him the judgment seat, and remind him that he will have to give an account of things done in the body. Labor to arouse the conscience; and pray God the Holy Spirit to work by you till the heart becomes tender and the mind perceives the need of the great salvation."[2]

Billy Graham said, "If our children grow up with no understanding of right and wrong...no desire to live with integrity...no faith in God...their souls will be impoverished, and they will miss life's highest good."[3]

Preface

It has been a joy to speak to children in camps and churches for thirty-five years. This volume contains some of my most effective sermons to children aged eight to twelve (many adaptable to teen audiences) complete with suggested props intended to assist ministers, parents, and children's workers in developing evangelistic/spiritual growth talks for children. Parents will find this volume a great resource for bedtime devotions and a teaching aid regarding Christian beliefs and practice for their children.

Effective evangelistic preaching to children hinges upon confidence (they *can* be saved); communication (clarity of need and way to be saved); conciseness (ten—fifteen minutes); and conservation (once they are saved). Experience has taught me that children can grasp biblical truth, even some deep theological truth, when couched in stories, illustrations and visuals. Such are windows to simplify and elucidate biblical truth; therefore, they are used frequently in these messages. Occasionally in addressing children, I use the big words of the church only to unpack them for understanding. In so doing, I introduce children to the beautiful and meaningful words of the faith that later they will embrace.

Included in this volume are sermons for special occasions—Easter, Christmas, Armed Forces Day, Thanksgiving, New Year's Day, Baptism and the Lord's Supper.

1
A Handful of Theology
Luke 1:4

Look at your hands. What do you see? Probably dirt. I want you to see something else—a handful of theology.[4] *Theology* is a big word which means the study of religious beliefs and practice.

The thumb stands for a theology of **God.** Since the thumb is the first finger of the hand, it is good to let it stand for God, who ought always to be first in our life. God is omnipotent; that is, He is all-powerful. God can do anything He wants to do, and no man or nation can stop Him.

God is omniscient; that is, He is all-knowing. There is nothing that God does not see. Has it ever occurred to you that nothing has ever occurred to God?

God is omnipresent; that is, He is present everywhere at the same time. He is with you and yet with the child in China. God is ever with you.

God is immutable; that is, He remains ever the same. "Jesus Christ the same yesterday, and to day, and for ever" (Hebrews 13:8).

God is love. God loves man and desires him to be saved (John 3:16). This love of God is uninfluenced by anything man has done or may do, and it is never-ending. "We love him, because he first loved us" (1 John 4:19).

The second finger stands for a theology of the **Bible.** The Bible is unique. There is no other Book like it. This Book is God's Word to man. It was written by 40 men over a period of 1,500 years. It consists of 66 books—39 in the Old

Testament and 27 in the New Testament. It is totally true in fact and doctrine. It has no contradictions. It is trustworthy.

The writer of Hebrews states: "The word of God is quick, and powerful, and sharper than any twoedged sword, piercing even to the dividing asunder of soul and spirit, and of the joints and marrow, and is a discerner of the thoughts and intents of the heart" (Hebrews 4:12). The Bible is fully alive; it is life-giving communication from God to man. It has power to convict man of sin and bring him to God. No other book in the world can do that. Nothing is said in the Bible that shouldn't have been said, and nothing which God wanted to include is missing.

I hope you can sing and will mean the rest of your life the song you learned in Vacation Bible School.

The B - I - B - L - E,
Yes it's the Book for me.
I stand alone on the Word of God—
The B - I - B - L – E!

Believe it against the opinion of any scientist, teacher, preacher, or friend. It is the Word of Him who cannot lie.

The tallest finger stands for a theology of **Sin and Satan.** Sin entered the human race in the Garden of Eden when Adam and Eve disobeyed God. Scripture states, "Wherefore, as by one man sin entered into the world, and death by sin; and so death passed upon all men, for that all have sinned" (Romans 5:12).

Sin is a failure to keep God's Law (Exodus 20) and any act that does not glorify God (1 Corinthians 10:31). In gist, sin is disobedience to the will of God which results in separation from God temporally and eternally, and "all have sinned" (Romans 3:23).

It is good for this finger to represent sin, for surprisingly, it is the weakest finger. Just ask any piano teacher. It speaks of our spiritual weakness (sin) and Satan's role both in our life and in the world.

This finger also represents the doctrine of Satan. He is a real personality. The Bible teaches that Satan possesses intelligence (2 Corinthians 11:3), emotions (Revelation 12:7), and a will (2 Timothy 2:26).

Satan's avowed purpose is to thwart the plan of God in every area, by every means possible. He may appear as a wily serpent or an attractive angel of light. He is the master deceiver, the wellspring of lies, the evil one, the tempter, a murderer, and the spoiler of good.

Far too long Satan has been the subject of fun instead of fear. There is no basis for presenting Satan with horns, tail, and hoofs! He is a tremendous foe, one which the believer must take seriously. Keep a proper attitude about Satan. Never assume that victory is automatic (Jude 8–9). Dress in the armor of God daily (Ephesians 6).

The ring finger stands for a theology of **Salvation.** It is fitting to attach salvation to the ring finger, for this doctrine is all about God's wondrous love for the world.

God loved the world so much that He sent His only Son to die upon a cross to make possible sin's forgiveness (John 3:16). Nothing short of Jesus' death, burial, and resurrection can atone for (forgive) man's sin. It is when man repents of sin (expresses godly sorrow for the sin of rejecting Christ, changes his mind about the role of Christ in his life) and exhibits faith (personal trust) in Jesus Christ that he is saved (Acts 20:21).

The little finger stands for a theology of **Last Things.** The Bible speaks of three events that will happen one day. The first is the *Return of Christ* to earth. In John 14, Jesus declared that He was going back to Heaven, but that He would return. In flying on a jet to Disney World, you could buy either a one-way ticket, which means you would stay there and not return, or you could buy a round-trip ticket, meaning you would go there for a little while and then come back. Jesus has a round-trip ticket. He went to Heaven for a little while, but soon He will return.

The second event is that of *Judgment.* There will be a day when the people who love Jesus and those who do not will face God's judgment. In every courtroom in America, there is a Judge who sits on a bench and makes people take responsibility for their actions. God will do the same.

Next, the Bible speaks of two eternal abodes: *Heaven and Hell* (Luke 16:22–23). Heaven is a place reserved for those who love Jesus Christ, while Hell is a place of punishment for those who do not. God's will is for every boy and girl to go to Heaven.

Review the handful of theology often with a friend so you will not to forget, and use it to help others understand the Christian faith.

Prop: A large drawing of a hand. Upon each finger, inscribe the appropriate point of theology it represents. Keep each finger covered until its truth is shared. In small settings, the use of your own hand will work effectively.

2
Shoes That Preach
I Peter 2:21

Various shoes teach spiritual truths about how a person should live for Jesus.

Dress Shoes speak of church attendance. Some call these shoes "Sunday-go-to-meeting shoes." You probably have some like them in the closet. These shoes remind us of the importance of going to church.

You are little in stature and faith and in need of others to help you grow in understanding of the Bible and Jesus. The gigantic Redwood trees have shallow roots. Roots are like anchors to a tree. They keep it from falling to the ground.

How then can these huge trees stand and not fall with shallow roots? Redwood trees intertwine their roots with each other, and therefore each draws strength from the others to stand. You have shallow roots spiritually that will cause a fall. Allow the roots of Christians in the church to wrap around yours and make you strong. We all need believers to assist us in our spiritual growth.

Swimming Shoes speak of baptism. These shoes are worn by swimmers and teach the importance of following Jesus in baptism following salvation. Baptism says the same two things as the wedding band on my finger. First, the band states that I love somebody and her name is Mary. Baptism says you love somebody, and His name is Jesus. Second, the ring says I belong to somebody, and her name is Mary. Baptism declares to Satan and the world that you belong to Jesus. Upon receiving Jesus as Lord and Savior, talk with your parents and pastor about being baptized.

Work Shoes speak of service. The apostle Paul wrote, "We are [God's] workmanship, created...unto good works" (Ephesians 2:10). These shoes teach the importance of working for Jesus.

You say, "Mr. Frank, I'm just a kid. What can I do for Jesus?" I'm sure that's what the little boy with the five loaves and two fishes thought. But Jesus used his fives and twos to feed 15,000–20,000 people. Little is much when God is in it.

Will you allow God to use your "fives and twos" to do His work? You have two hands with five fingers each, two feet with five toes each, two eyes, two ears, and two lips. Use these fives and twos working for Jesus in whatever ways possible.

Use your fives and twos spending time with a lonely person, visiting the elderly at the nursing home brightening their day, assisting the teacher in class, and earning money and giving it to missions. Your little can count for much, just as the loaves and fishes of the little boy did.

School Shoes speak of study. Your mother will take you to the store before school begins to buy school shoes. School is a place to study and learn. These shoes are a reminder of the need to study the Bible on our own. It's good to go to church and have others teach the Bible to you, but that's no substitute for studying it personally.

At Yellowstone National Park, dozens of small bears die each winter after tourist season, waiting along the highway for a handout. No one comes to feed them, resulting in their death. Don't be like the small bears waiting upon others to feed you the Bible. Wear these shoes every day, learning about Jesus and His plan for your life.

Play Shoes speak of fun. In putting these shoes on, you know some serious fun is about to happen! I want these shoes to serve as a reminder of God's desire for you to have fun living for Him. Living for Jesus is not a dull, drab thing (John 10:10). Don't let Satan rob you of the joy God wants you to experience in the Christian life.

Bedroom Shoes speak of laziness. People wear these kinds of shoes when they want to be lazy and lie around the house. Shoes like these warn us not to be lazy in living for Jesus by obeying and serving Him. The church has plenty of lazy saints. Don't become one of them.

Soccer Shoes speak of steadfastness. Soccer shoes have cleats which help soccer players have good footing, so they will not slip or fall down easily in playing soccer. Wear spiritual shoes like these to stand firm for Jesus. Never allow others to persuade you to do something that is wrong or cause you to fail to obey the Lord.

Shadrach, Meshach, and Abednego wore "shoes" like these when they refused to bow down to the 90-foot statue made by Nebuchadnezzar. In response to their stand, the king ordered them to be cast into a fiery furnace, from which God delivered them unharmed (Daniel 3:13–27). These men stood firm for God, even though it could have cost them their lives.

Always be like them, standing true to Jesus. Though the stars fall from the sky, never bend or bow to the pressures of the world to stop living for Jesus.

Running Shoes speak of discipline. It takes discipline, determination and passion to be a runner. To live for Jesus takes the same attitude spiritually. Each day, work hard at being the best Christian possible by practicing a daily quiet time and obeying God.

Running shoes also speak of the need to exercise physically to care for the body, which is the Temple of God.

7

Shorten the time spent in front of the television or computer in order to engage in activities outside like football, baseball, or hopscotch.

Advertising Shoes [Tootsie-Roll flip-flops] speak of telling. That Tootsie-Roll shoes advertise for Tootsie-Roll is clear, for the name Tootsie-Roll is all over them. It makes me want one right now. Let your life be advertising shoes for Jesus, both showing and telling of the love of Jesus. May your life make others want to know Jesus (Acts 1:8).

Remember the lesson of the shoes, and be sure to wear them all the time. If you have not put on the gospel shoes of salvation by asking Jesus into your heart, do that right now.

Prop: A tub with the type of shoes symbolizing each point. Hold up the type of shoe that is under discussion at each point.

3
Dead-End Roads
Proverbs 14:12

Many roads lead to a dead end regarding our happiness, our peace, our walk with God, and our highest good.

One of the roads that lead to a dead end is **Whiskey Road.** Television describes drinking alcohol as a cool thing, failing to tell the audience that alcohol damages glands in the body, destroys brain cells, and shortens life.

Drinking alcohol is a dead end to God's best plan for your life. Daniel "purposed in his heart that he would not defile himself with the portion of the king's meat, nor with the wine which he drank" (Daniel 1:8). Determine to be a Daniel staying off this road.

Porn Circle is a dead end. Pornography, a thirteen-billion-dollar business in America, is presented in bad magazines and sexually explicit movies. There are three times as many porn video stores and adult book houses in America as McDonald's restaurants, and there are at least 100,000 pornography websites. Stay off this road by refusing to look at any website, magazine, or video that shows bad pictures. Say with David, "I will set no wicked thing before mine eyes" (Psalm 101:3).

Drug Street is a dead end. Drugs (LSD, marijuana, cocaine, etc.) kill. Len Bias was a basketball star at the University of Maryland. He signed a multimillion-dollar contract with the Boston Celtics and had product endorse-ments. In celebration of the signing, a contract party was hosted at which he took a slug of pure cocaine for the first time. It killed him. Don't listen to the lie of Satan that one-time drug use won't hurt you. It could kill you. Don't walk down this street; stay well off it.

Tobacco Avenue is a dead end. One in four adult smokeless tobacco users began between the age of five and eight. An additional twenty-five percent of users began between the ages of nine and twelve. Smokeless tobacco increases the chance of cancer of the cheek and gums fiftyfold. A tobacco company salesman said regarding smokeless tobacco, "Once a kid's hooked, he doesn't leave."

Say NO to cigarette smoking also, because it damages health and shortens life. God tells us not to consume anything that damages the body, for it is the "temple of the Holy Spirit" (I Corinthians 6:19). Don't chew or light up!

Wrong Friend Boulevard is a dead end. The Bible states, "He that walketh with wise men shall be wise: but a companion of fools shall be destroyed" (Proverbs 13:20). Choose friends cautiously and biblically. It has been said rightly, "On thy choice of friends, thy good or evil depends."

Pure and clean water passing through a dirty pipe will become dirty. What happens when a good apple is placed next to a rotten apple? Does the good apple cause the rotten apple to become good? No, but the rotten apple causes the good apple to become bad.

People become like those with whom they hang out. Choose friends who love Jesus, love His Word and live right (Psalm 119:63). Stay off Wrong Friend Boulevard, for it is a dead end to real happiness.

Dishonesty Lane is a dead end. Honesty is not only the best policy; it is the only policy. Always be honest and truthful. Never tell a lie, cheat on a test, or steal.

Sex Highway is a dead end. One-half of twelve-year-olds in America testify of already having engaged in sex. Sex is something God created for a husband and wife, and it is wrong outside of the bonds of marriage. Remain pure and clean sexually until you are married.

Conformity Drive is a dead end. *Conformity* is a big word. In this case, it means "to become like the people who don't love God."

Paul declared, "I beseech you therefore, brethren, by the mercies of God, that ye present your bodies a living sacrifice, holy, acceptable unto God, which is your reasonable service. And be not conformed to this world: but be ye transformed" (Romans 12:1–2).

In a day when bobbed hair was the fashion for girls, two daughters of a southern governor insisted that they have their hair fixed in that way. After hearing this, the father said, "You are the daughters of a governor. You don't follow the styles. You set the styles."

You are the children of the King of Heaven. You don't follow the styles and trends of this wicked world; God has called us to set them. Don't conform to the pressure to be like those who don't love Jesus.

Instead of traveling the bad roadways of Satan, choose to travel the Good Road that God has provided. Go God's way, which leads to sure happiness, peace, hope, and Heaven (John 14:6).

Prop: "Dead-End Street" sign; street signs made for each "dead end" discussed, on boards the size of street signs and painted green (use alphabet stickers for names); a "God's Way" street sign; Plastic Tack to fasten street signs to "Dead-End Street" sign; two three-inch PVC pipes inserted in a concrete circular mold for mounting bases for the two signs.

Attach street signs to the "Dead-End Street" sign in the order shared. In the closing challenge, urge the children to stay off all the roads that lead to a dead end, remaining constantly on the road that leads to God's best (display the "God's Way" sign).

4

A Wedding Ceremony and Salvation
Romans 9:10–13

Marriage preaches the message of salvation in the way it begins and ends.

The first step to marriage requires an **introduction.** Two people must each know that the other exists before they ever can get married. People don't fall in love with someone they don't know.

This is the first step in getting married, and the same is true about salvation. Before you can trust Jesus as Lord and Savior, someone must introduce you to Him. Prayerfully, that is what this sermon is doing. Christians should ever be introducing others to Him. The Bible calls this witnessing (Acts 1:8).

The second step to marriage is **dating.** A person wants to know all about a person before marrying him or her. In dating, a couple learns about each other's likes, dislikes, beliefs, plans, and whether or not it is God's will for them to marry.

This is also true in regard to Jesus Christ. A person needs to know who Jesus is and what He wants of them before saying "I do" to the offer of salvation. This "dating" time with Jesus can be short or long, depending on how much time one spends seeking to know Him.

A boy who fails to make a diligent effort to get to know a girl will not succeed in that relationship. The same is true for anyone who fails to make a good effort to get to know Jesus. The reason why many have not become Christians is that they

13

failed to make an effort to understand who Jesus is, what He did for them, and why He did it.

The third step to marriage is **walking the aisle.** It is common for Mendelssohn's "Here comes the bride" to play as the bride walks down the aisle to marry the groom. I have seen many brides make this walk with face aglow and heart pounding.

Often people walk the aisle in church to the song "Just As I Am" with face aglow and heart pounding to give their life to Jesus Christ. If Christ speaks to your heart in a service, you should step out and do the same as soon as the invitation is given.

The fourth step to marriage is the **wedding ceremony.** The minister asks the couple to promise to love and care for each other until death. Upon their agreement, he asks, "Do you take this man/woman to be your husband/wife for life?" They respond, "I do." It is at this moment that they are married. Walking down the aisle didn't make them married. Men and women have walked down the aisle to the wedding altar and changed their minds about getting married. They left the church unmarried.

In the same way, one is not saved simply by walking down the aisle to the preacher during the singing of a song. One must say "I do" to Jesus' offer of salvation. Sadly, many have walked down the aisle to the salvation altar and failed to invite Jesus into their heart, leaving the church yet unsaved.

Fifth, wedding rings are exchanged. What do people give each other when they get married? A wedding ring. I am wearing one on my hand. The wedding ring says three things: I love someone, I belong to someone, and I am committed to the one I married forever.

The wedding ring the Christian wears following salvation is baptism. It tells the world loudly and clearly of his or her relationship to Jesus.

A wedding ring doesn't make a person married, and neither does baptism make someone a Christian. I wear a wedding ring because I am not ashamed of my union to my wife. Believers certainly are not ashamed of the fact that Jesus is their Savior, so they are gladly baptized.

The **marriage license** is a sixth part of a marriage. The bride and groom sign a document stating that they indeed were married on a certain date. This document is put on file in the courthouse as a historical record.

When a person gets saved, his or her name is written down, recorded in the Lamb's Book of Life in Heaven by God.

Next, a **celebration reception** takes place. Finally, after a long wait due to wedding photos being taken of the bride and groom, it's time to dig in to some good food and cake. This is called the wedding reception. At the wedding reception, congratulations are shared by family and friends with the couple just married. The wedding reception is a time of celebration.

The Bible tells us that when a person gets saved, it makes news in Heaven, and a celebration breaks out in the presence of the angels (Luke 15:10)!

The last parts of the marriage are the honeymoon and new home. Upon returning from their honeymoon, do the newlyweds go back to live with their parents? Absolutely not, for they now can no longer live as they once did. Marriage changes things.

Upon receiving Christ, a person's life is forever changed. It will never again be the same. Paul states that when a person receives Jesus, "old things are passed away; behold, all things are become new" (2 Corinthians 5:17). An old song says it best. "It's different now, since Jesus saved my soul. It's different now, since Jesus made me whole. Old Satan had to flee, when Jesus rescued me. Now it's different, oh, so different now."[5]

Are you ready to say "I do" to Jesus' offer of forgiveness of sin and eternal life?[6]

Prop: Large posters prepared to illustrate each point. Hold the poster that parallels the point being made.

5
The Colors of Salvation
John 3:16

Various colors present the Gospel.

Black stands for man's sin against God. Sin is disobeying God. It is failing to keep His commandments. "For all have sinned and fall short of the glory of God" (Romans 3:23 NASB).

Sin has the power to separate a person from God now and in eternity. Sin also hinders a person from experiencing God's best intentions for life.

Everyone's greatest need is salvation—forgiveness of sin. But how do we get this?

Red stands for the precious blood of Jesus Christ. It is impossible for man to save himself from the consequences of sin. But Jesus Christ is able.

John says, "The blood of Jesus Christ his Son cleanseth us from all sin" (I John 1:7). John 3:16 declares, "For God so loved the world (you), that he gave his only begotten Son, that whosoever (you) believeth in him should not perish, but have everlasting life." God gave His only Son to the death of a Cross to bear man's sin so that man might be reconciled (saved) to God.

White stands for cleansing of sin. The condition for salvation (forgiveness) is "repentance toward God, and faith toward our Lord Jesus Christ" (Acts 20:21).

To repent is to change one's mind about both the sin which he has committed and the place he gives God in life. The moment a person turns from sin to the Lord Jesus Christ, receiving Him as Lord and Savior, new life begins.

God says "Come now, and let us reason together..., though your sins be as scarlet, they shall be as white as snow; though they be red like crimson, they shall be as wool" (Isaiah 1:18). When we bring our personal sins to Jesus Christ, He forgives them, making us a child of God, white as snow on the inside!

Blue stands for confession of Christ openly in believers' baptism. Baptism does not save a person; one is baptized because of salvation. Baptism is a bold declaration to the world that a person believes in Jesus' death, burial, and resurrection and testifies of reception of Him as Lord and Savior.

Baptism is the very first order of business for the new Christian. Jesus declared, "Whosoever therefore shall confess me before men, him will I confess also before my Father which is in heaven. But whosoever shall deny me before men, him will I also deny before my Father which is in heaven" (Matthew 10:32–33).

I wear a wedding band because I am unashamedly married to Mary, not to become married to her. Likewise, one is baptized because he is unashamedly saved, not in order to be saved.

Green stands for the disciplines essential for spiritual growth. Once a person receives Christ as Savior and Lord, he is as a "newborn babe," requiring help to grow up in Christ Jesus (1 Peter 2:2; 2 Peter 3:18). The Christian grows through Bible study, prayer, church attendance (worship and fellowship with the saints), and witnessing.

Purple stands for the Lordship of Christ in the believer's life. Jesus is to be Lord of all. As Lord, He has the say-so about every detail of life.

Yellow stands for the saint's faithful service to Jesus Christ. Christians are to be "faithful unto death" in their service and in their stand for the Lord (Revelation 2:10). Sadly, more people start out as great saints than end up as great saints. Remain faithful to Christ throughout life.

Gold stands for the believer's eternal home in Heaven. Heaven awaits the child of God at the end of life's journey.

Gray stands for the "Valley of Decision," in which many reside. The prophet Joel cries, "Multitudes, multitudes in the valley of decision: for the day of the LORD is near in the valley of decision" (Joel 3:14).

The Lord calls on man to make a decision concerning personal sin and his relationship to Him. I paraphrase Pilate's question in Matthew 27:22: "What will you do with Jesus?" You cannot remain neutral.

Right now, Jesus is "knocking on the door of your heart" seeking entrance. He says, "Behold, I stand at the door, and knock: if any man hear my voice, and open the door, I will come in to him, and will sup with him, and he with me" (Revelation 3:20).

Will you open that door by faith and repentance, receiving His free gift of eternal life? Jesus promises that if you will open the door, He will come in!

Prop: Seven regular-size posterboards colored to match each point of the talk. Laminated Colors of Salvation cards (wallet size) are available from this ministry.

6
Put a Ring on His Hand
Luke 15:22

A boy left home and did some very bad things. He became sorry for what he had done and headed for home. His Father, in seeing him walking down the road to their house, ran to meet him. One thing the father instructed a servant to do was to "put a ring on his hand." What a wondrous welcome home he received!

There are golden rings, pearl rings, diamond rings, college rings, friendship rings, and true-love-waits rings; but the most prized ring is the one Jesus puts on the hand of the person He forgives. I'm not talking about a real ring like the one I wear on my hand, but a spiritual one that is worn upon the heart.

What kind of ring does Jesus put on our hand spiritually upon salvation?

It is a **Ring of Acceptance.** Jesus accepts the sinner, regardless of the sins he has committed. The apostle Paul declares, "He [God] hath made us accepted in the beloved" (Ephesians 1:6).

It is a **Ring of Affection.** In the marriage ceremony, couples exchange rings which speak of their love for each other. It is fitting that the father in the story says, "Put a ring on his hand," for it speaks of his great love for the returning son.

When we trust Jesus as Lord and Savior, He places the ring of affection upon the hand of the new believer, for it speaks of His wondrous love. "For God so loved the world, that he gave his only begotten Son, that whosoever believeth in him should not perish, but have everlasting life" (John 3:16).

Karl Barth stated that the greatest truth of Scripture is "Jesus loves me; this I know, for the Bible tells me so."

It is a **Ring of Acquittal.** *Acquittal* is a big word which means "forgiveness." The act of the father placing a ring on his son's hand said loudly and clearly, "I forgive you." The moment Jesus is received as Lord and Savior, sin is totally forgiven.

As a teacher uses an eraser to clean a chalkboard of mistakes made, Jesus completely erases a person's sin with His precious blood. The third stanza of an all-time favorite hymn of mine ("It Is Well with My Soul") states:

> My sin, oh, the bliss of this glorious thought,
> My sin, not in part, but the whole,
> Is nailed to the cross, and I bear it no more.
> Praise the Lord; praise the Lord, oh, my soul![7]

It is a Ring of Adoption. At salvation a person is placed into the family of God as an adopted son. How awesome! John exclaims,

> *"Behold, what manner of love the Father hath bestowed upon us, that we should be called the sons of God: therefore the world knoweth us not, because it knew him not.*
> *" Beloved, now are we the sons of God, and it doth not yet appear what we shall be: but we know that, when he shall appear, we shall be like him; for we shall see him as he is. "*
> —1 John 3:1–2.

Every person, upon becoming a Christian, can say, "I'm a child of the King, a child of the King. With Jesus my Savior, I'm a child of the King."[8]

How great it would be to be the child of a king, a president, or a millionaire; but none of these compares with being a child of God!

It is a **Ring of Assurance.** A ring of gold is an unbroken, continuous circle and speaks of everlasting love, unconditional love. In saying, "Put a ring upon his hand," the father was vowing to always love his son and include him in the family.

Jesus' ring states the same truth for all His children. Jesus' love is unconditional—no strings attached. The ring loudly states that once a person is a child of God, he is always, from that time, a child of God. When you doubt Jesus' love, look at the promise ring upon your finger placed there by God.

Jesus longs to place the spiritual ring just described on your hand. He left Heaven to do it. He died upon a cruel cross to do it. He was raised from the dead to do it. He ever knocks upon your heart's door to do it. Why not let Jesus do it now?

Prop: Various types of rings, including a gold wedding band.

7
How to Pack Your Suitcase for Life
Matthew 7:21–27

In preparation for going home tomorrow, do a good job in packing your suitcase with everything you brought to camp. It will make both Mom and the camp staff happy.

You need also to do a good job of packing your *heart suitcase,* because you will be living out of it for the rest of your life. There are several things that ought to be packed in this suitcase, things that will enable life to be lived at its fullest and will prevent spiritual straying.

Pack your **Decision Card.** What decision did you make this week for Christ? Was it for salvation, surrender to full time Christian ministry, to witness to a friend or to avoid the Dead End Roads or to be baptized? Take that decision home and live it out. It will do you no good to leave it here.

Pack a **Fence Concerning Friends.** Wrong friends will cause you to stumble spiritually; therefore, select as friends those who love God devotedly. Say as David did, "I am a companion of all them that fear thee, and of them that keep thy precepts" (Psalm 119:63). Pack a fence to keep out injurious friends.

Pack the **Bible.** Don't forget to pack the Word of God; don't leave your Bible at camp. Take it home to read and obey every day. The Bible nourishes and strengthens the heart and provides guidance.

Pack your **Memories.** Pack camp photos and the camp DVD. Photos of friends, staffers, and leaders will remind you in difficult days of how much you are loved and appreciated, and that, regardless of what is faced in life, you *don't have to* *face it alone.* Photos also will be a reminder that the Christian life is not a boring, dull deal, but one that is filled with fun and laughter.

Pack the **Cross.** Don't leave this point in your life without Jesus Christ.

In Matthew 7, Jesus tells the story about two house builders. One of these builders built his house upon the sand, while the other built his upon the rock. In time, a storm came and blew against these two houses. The house built upon the sand was destroyed, while the house built upon the rock stood.

These two houses picture life. Life built upon the shifting sands of pleasure, possessions, and wrongdoing in time will collapse *(great will be the fall of it),* whereas life built upon the rock Jesus Christ will stand firm regardless of the storms encountered.

What will you do with Jesus? Will you accept Him or reject Him, crown Him Lord of your life or crucify Him, be for Him or against Him, be His friend or be His foe, say yes to Him or no to Him?

There is no neutral ground. *You will leave camp with Christ in your heart suitcase or yet outside of it.* Make sure you leave knowing Him personally. A personal relationship with Jesus is foundational for happiness today and in eternity.

Pack **Prayer.** Prayer is a must to be packed, for it is the key to victorious Christian living. Talk often to God, requesting that His supernatural power be released in and through your life so you may overcome temptation and live rightly.

Pack a **Bottle of Mouthwash.** Keep your mouth clean from uttering unkind and hurtful words. Speak words that build up others, not words that tear them down. Speak words that tell the gospel story.

Pack a **Helmet.** A helmet reminds you to guard your thoughts, keeping them pure and clean. Thoughts determine, to large degree, what will shape all of the rest of life. With this in mind, the apostle Paul said, "Finally, brethren, whatsoever things are true, whatsoever things are honest, whatsoever things are just, whatsoever things are pure, whatsoever things are lovely, whatsoever things are of good report; if there be any virtue, and if there be any praise, think on these things" (Philippians 4:8).

Pack **Earplugs.** Pack earplugs as a reminder not to listen to negative people—people who seek to discourage you from following God. David wore spiritual earplugs when he was told not to fight Goliath. He listened to God instead of man and defeated the giant (1 Samuel 17:29).

Pack a **Bar of Soap.** A bar of soap is a reminder of the need to stay clean spiritually. God's bar of soap is 1 John 1:9 and 1 John 1:7. You will need to use it often in life.

Pack a **Twenty-Dollar Bill.** I asked three students if they wanted a twenty-dollar bill which I held in my hand. They all did. I then took the bill, crushed it up in my hands, and again asked who wanted it. Again all responded in the affirmative. Next, tossing the bill onto the floor, I squashed it with my shoe. With the bill in my hand, I inquired again who still wanted it, and not one said they didn't. "Why do you," I asked, "still want this crushed up, wrinkled up and soiled bill?"

A twelve-year-old girl answered, "Because it hasn't lost its value." Wow! What a good answer! Despite the condition of the twenty-dollar bill, it had not lost its value. Its blemishes had not altered its worth.

Your life is like the twenty-dollar bill. Your value to God is not based upon what happens to you, but upon the fact that He made you in His own image. He cannot love you any more or less than He does now, for His love never changes. He will love you when you're up or when you're down, when you're in or when you're out, when you're soaring high spiritually or when you have a crash.

Never forget that God's love is not dependent upon your performance or popularity or great intellect. It is an unconditional love. No yardstick can measure God's love; it cannot be fully described or defined, just accepted and experienced. This is why the apostle Paul said, "And may you have the power to understand, as all God's people should, how wide, how long, how high, and how deep his love is. May you experience the love of Christ, though it is too great to understand fully. Then you will be made complete with all the fullness of life and power that comes from God" (Ephesians 3:18–19, NLT).

Will you pack these items in your life's heart suitcase? Success or failure, joy or sorrow, shipwreck or victory will be pretty much determined by how you pack this suitcase and daily live out of it. I urge you to put each of these objects in your suitcase and then zip it up all the way. You will be living out of this suitcase, and you will need each item it contains until you get to Heaven.

Prop: A suitcase, a bed, chest of drawers and objects to symbolize each item to pack (in the chest of drawers). Take objects from the chest of drawers and pack in the suitcase as discussed. This talk may easily be adapted for a New Year's challenge.

8
John 3:16 Sent Me
John 3:16

I want you to imagine a story that takes place in a northern state in the midst of winter.[9] It is frigid cold outside and snowing; icicles are hanging from the rafters of homes and buildings. A policeman is making his nightly rounds in a squad car, when he hears a disturbance in an alley. He stops the car, and with a megaphone, he says, "Whoever is in there, come out right now." The noise stops. As he begins to drive away, the noise recurs. The officer stops the car, gets out, and proceeds toward the trash cans in the alley. In pointing the beam of a flashlight upon the trash cans, he says, "This is your final chance. Come out right now." A trash can lid lifts up with a small boy standing beneath it. The boy is barefoot, wearing clothes that are tattered and torn. The policeman, upon instructing the boy to get out of the trashcan, asks, "What were you doing in there anyway?"

The boy answers, "I was cold and was trying to get warm. I was hungry and was trying to find something to eat. I was lost and was trying to find a place to spend the night." The policeman, with compassion, pointed to a rescue mission where the boy could find help. The boy objected, "Nobody in this town has been willing to help me. Why will those people help, when others didn't?"

The policeman said, "These folks are different. Just tell them John 3:16 sent you."

With some reluctance, the boy walked down the sidewalk to the mission and knocked on the door. A big man opened the door and asked if he could be of help. The boy said,

"John 3:16 sent me." Immediately the man welcomed the boy into the mission. The boy warmed his chilled body by the fireplace, took a bath, put on clean clothes, enjoyed a wondrous meal, and then got a good night's sleep.

In the morning, the snow had stopped falling, the sun was shining, and the birds were chirping, as he began to walk down the steps from the rescue mission. He looked back over his shoulder just long enough to say, "I sure don't know what John 3:16 is, but it sure can get a cold boy warm."

There is something warm and cozy about the love of God. It warms me to know that my wife and my children love me. It warms me to know that I have friends who love me. But greater than all of this is knowing that God loves me. Wow! To know that the God of all creation loves me blows my mind and fills me with warmth like nothing else can. But He doesn't love just me; He loves the entire world. "For God so loved the world"—not a nation, not just good people or a certain color of people, but all people.

A great preacher named Karl Barth once was asked what he thought was the greatest truth of all Scripture. He stunned many, no doubt, by answering, "Jesus loves me; this I know, for the Bible tells me so." God loves you. Another minister named Augustine stated, "God loves each one of us as if we were the only one to love." Understand that God's love is not like an apple pie that mom serves at supper from which Dad gets a big piece and you get a small piece. No. God gives each of us the "whole pie" of His love. He does not love me any more than He loves you; He loves us equally.

C. H. Spurgeon, one of history's greatest pastors, visited a farm. He saw a weather vane that bore the inscription, "God is love." He asked the farmer if he meant by that inscription that God's love changes with the wind. He answered, "No. I mean that whichever direction the wind blows, God's love remains the same." God loves you with an everlasting love. He will love you when you are good and when you are not so good. There will never be a time when God will stop loving you. There may come a time when your father or mother stop loving you, but not so with God. Never equate God's love with the love of a parent or a friend.

You ask, "How can I know God loves me?" Just look to the cross. God loved you so much that He gave His one and only Son to die on the cross to make possible your salvation. If, after chapel, I saw a speeding car approaching you, I would push you out of the way, even if it meant dying in your place. I love you that much. But I don't know any of you that I would let my only son die for. You see, it would be easier for me to die for you than to let him die for you. But that is exactly what God did for us. He sent His only Son, Jesus, to die on the cross so we might live forever. If that isn't love, then the ocean is dry, and the sky is not blue. How amazing and awesome the love of God is for us!

A second thing that the poor boy said as he left the rescue mission that day was, "I don't know what John 3:16 is, but it sure can get a dirty boy clean." He was filthy, but with the help of Dial soap and water, he got clean.

Scripture makes it plain that just as the body gets dirty on the outside, hearts get dirty due to sin on the inside. Dial soap cannot wash sin away; only Jesus Christ can do that. When you bring your dirty sin to Jesus, He will wash it clean through His blood, making you white as snow on the inside. An old hymn underscores this great truth: "Whiter than snow, yes, whiter than snow—now wash me, and I shall be whiter than snow."

As he left the rescue mission looking back over his shoulder, the boy also said, "I don't know what John 3:16 is, but it sure can get a hungry boy fed." He was starving but was able to sit down to feast on all kind of delicious food.

Did you know that inside all of us is a hunger for God? Not all recognize that hunger as being for God. Some try to satisfy that hunger with beer, drugs, pornography, material possessions, and pleasure. But these things can't, for only Jesus can satisfy the soul. A song we used to sing here at camp said, "There is a hole in my heart that cannot be filled with the things that I do. There is a hole in my heart that can only be filled with You." The song is scripturally correct. You have a God-shaped hole in your heart that only Jesus can fill. In receiving Jesus into the heart, you receive His peace and joy that satisfies as nothing else.

A final thing he said as he left the rescue mission was, "I don't know what John 3:16 is, but it sure can get a lost boy found." He was lost but got direction to find his way home.

John 3:16 tells us that all people are lost, but in Christ Jesus, we can be found. Jesus will guide our footsteps throughout life's journey until we reach Heaven, preventing us from ever getting lost again. Now that you understand John 3:16 better say that verse aloud. Would you like for Jesus to become your Lord and Savior?

Prop: A flashlight; trashcan with lid; globe (to illustrate the 'world'); blanket (Cold boy warm); bar of soap, four color shirts to illustrate salvation (Dirty boy clean); plate with fork (hungry boy fed); and a map (Lost boy found).

9
Baptism
Matthew 28:18–20

The first thing a child is to do after becoming a Christian is to be baptized. This lesson will help you understand what baptism is and why you need to be baptized.

What Baptism Says for the Saint. My wedding band says loudly two things. It declares that I love somebody, Mary, my wife; and that I belong to somebody, Mary, my wife.

Baptism states the same things. It says to friends, family, and others that I belong to and love Jesus Christ. Baptism tells people what happened in your life upon receiving Christ as Savior. Going under the water pictures how Jesus washed your sins away. Coming up out of the water speaks of your new life in Christ.

As the wedding ring is a symbol of marital union, so baptism is a symbol of one's union with Christ. I am not married simply because I wear the ring. A person may wear a ring and not be married. In the same way, a person who is not saved does not become a Christian by being baptized. It is possible to be baptized and not be a child of God. Scripture is clear that before a person is baptized, he is to be saved.

What Baptism Says about the Savior. Baptism is a picture of what happened to Jesus on Good Friday through Easter morning.

As the minister lowers a person into the water in baptism, it tells of Jesus' death on the Cross to save man from the penalty of sin. Being under the water speaks of Jesus' being in the grave for three days, and coming up out of the water shows Jesus' resurrection. Baptism tells of what Jesus did before, on, and after the cross.

Jesus suffered much due to His love for the world (crown of thorns, sword-pierced side, beating with the Roman cat o' nine tails, and crucifixion). Prior to Jesus' death on the cross, He cried, "Father, forgive them; for they know not what they do" concerning His murderers. The body of Jesus was buried, and the tomb was sealed.

But what happened on the third day (Easter morning)? The stone was rolled away by God, and Jesus was raised from the dead. Jesus revealed Himself to people for the next forty days before going back to Heaven. Jesus will come back to earth to take all those who love Him to Heaven. Baptism says for Jesus, "I am he that liveth, and was dead; and, behold, I am alive for evermore, Amen; and have the keys of hell and of death" (Revelation 1:18).

What Baptism Says to the Sinner. Baptism not only speaks for the saint and about the Savior; it also speaks to the sinner. Baptism tells the message of God's awesome love for the world (John 3:16).

Baptism declares that the way God has made for man to be made right with Him is through the death, burial, and resurrection of Jesus, His only Son.

"For this is good and acceptable in the sight of God our Saviour;

"Who will have all men to be saved, and to come unto the knowledge of the truth.

"For there is one God, and one mediator between God and men, the man Christ Jesus;

"Who gave himself a ransom for all, to be testified in due time."—I Timothy 2:3–6.

Sin separated man from God, but Jesus became man's Mediator (bridge) to God.

What does the Bible say about baptism? The Bible says only those who are saved may be baptized; that immediately following conversion, one should be baptized; that the believer cannot live with a clear conscience if he or she is not baptized; that age is not a factor in relation to baptism, only salvation is; that there is only one true baptism, and that follows salvation; that biblical baptism occurs but once; and that baptism without salvation is without meaning.

There is no need to fear the step of baptism. The minister will gladly show you the baptistery and rehearse what will take place upon your baptism.

If you are a Christian but have never been baptized, I urge you to talk to your parents and pastor about this next step in your Christian walk.

Prop: Video projector to show video clips of a person being baptized or large clip-art of same.

10
Do You Know Jesus?
Matthew 7:22

Knowing *about* someone is not the same as *knowing* him or her. Who knows this person? (A photo of the President of the United States is shown to the children.) All of us know that it's the President of the United States. But what I am asking is how many *know* the President? Probably none of you do. It is different to know about the President and to know the President.

There is a difference between knowing about someone and knowing someone. Do you only know about Jesus, or do you really know Him?

Believing in someone is not the same as trusting him or her. A man named Blondie pushed a wheelbarrow on a tightrope over the Niagara Falls. The people cheered as he made it to the other side without falling.

He asked, "How many believe I can push someone in this wheelbarrow over the Falls?" The people shouted their belief that he could do it. He then asked, "Who of you is willing to be that person?" Nobody's hand went up.

Despite belief in his ability to accomplish the feat, none were willing to be the one in the wheel barrow. There is a difference between believing and trusting. People can believe that Jesus can save them, but until they trust Him (sit down in the wheelbarrow), they will remain unsaved.

Here is a chair. My brain tells me it is a chair, that the purpose of a chair is to hold a person up, and that this chair has done that many times. I believe it can hold me up, but it can do me no good until I trust it to fulfill its purpose by sitting on it.

The same is true with salvation. We can believe that Jesus can save us, wash away our sins, and one day take us to Heaven; but not until we "sit down in the chair," trusting Him, will we be saved.

Liking someone is not the same as loving someone. Many people like Jesus as a Teacher but don't love Him as their Savior. These people seek to live by His teaching about love, forgiveness, helping others, and doing good deeds; but they don't love Him.

Simply obeying Jesus is not synonymous with loving Jesus. One can keep the Ten Commandments, attend church, tithe, and be baptized without loving Jesus.

Saying that you belong to someone is not the same as belonging to him or her. A lot of people claim that they belong to Jesus, that they are Christians, who are not really saved. Jesus said, "Many will say to me in that day, Lord, Lord,…then will I profess unto them, I never knew you" (Matthew 7:22–23). Just saying you belong to Jesus doesn't mean you actually do.

How does a person become a child of God? Acts 20:21 indicates that it is through repentance (expression of sorrow for one's sin and a desire to change) and faith (trust) in the Lord Jesus Christ.

Prop: A photo of the President of the United States of America.

11
Golf and the Gospel
Matthew 7:13–14

The game of golf illustrates the Christian life.

Look at **the course we must play.** Golfers have thousands of courses on which they may play—some easy, while others are difficult. These courses have sand traps, water holes, and narrow fairways, making play difficult.

The Christian has only one course to play, and that is the course of this evil and sinful world (I John 5:19). This course is most difficult, having all kinds of traps—obstacles seeking to cause us to live poorly. Included in these traps are disobedience to God and parents, alcohol, drugs, bad magazines and movies, and wrong friends.

Prior to playing a course, a good golfer thoroughly studies its obstacles and most difficult holes. This study enables him to prepare to face every challenge confronted.

A good Christian studies what the Bible indicates he will face during the course of life in order to be prepared to overcome the traps Satan has set for him (1 Peter 5:8; Psalm 141:9).

Consider **the clubs we must use.** Most golf bags contain various kinds of irons and woods, each designed to help the golfer play his best. Golf clubs, however, cannot help the golfer until he learns how and when to use them.

The Christian has spiritual clubs (Bible, prayer, church, Holy Spirit, Christian friends) to enable and enhance his walk with God. He must learn how and when to use.

There are **the rules we must obey.** The golfer cannot play in any way that he wants to. Golfers have a rule book to govern play (PGA rules). Dean Wilson was disqualified for failure to sign his scorecard after the second round of play in the Buick Invitational in 2005. He failed to play by the rules.

Neither can the Christian "play" in any manner which he chooses. The Christian's rule book is the Holy Bible. The Christian must play by all the rules, lest he become "disqualified" from receiving the reward he seeks.

Think about **the discipline (hard effort) you must exert.** No golfer can play at his best without constant practice and discipline. It takes persistent hard work to be a successful golfer like Tiger Woods. No professional golfer ever is satisfied; he always wants to improve performance.

The Apostle Paul says, "Work out your own salvation with fear and trembling" (Philippians 2:12). We must work hard at pleasing God every day, striving to live better for Him than we did on the previous day.

There is **a goal we must seek.** Par is the worthy goal of the golfer, for it means he has mastered the course. Anything better than par is icing on the cake.

Par in the Christian life is doing the will of God in regard to our conduct and career. It is living a life well-pleasing in His sight.

Don't forget **the bad shots we must play.** Ted Williams was a great baseball player, and Sam Snead was a great golfer. One day these men were discussing which sport was the hardest. Williams told Snead that in baseball, the batter had to hit a ball hurled ninety miles an hour while contending with crowd noise, but in golf, one simply has to stand before a silent crowd and hit a still ball. Snead responded, "Yes, that's true, but we have to play our foul balls too."

Christians have to play their foul balls—their mistakes, sins, blunders, and poor decisions. Any time you make a bad shot (do wrong), God stands ready to forgive, enabling play to resume.

Ultimately, **the last hole must be played.** The game of golf is not over until all eighteen holes have been played. The great golfers play their best until the very end. Even those who don't come in first receive a better prize for coming in higher.

The eighteenth hole for Christians is completed when they depart for Heaven. The apostle Paul said,

"I have fought a good fight, I have finished my course, I have kept the faith:

"Henceforth there is laid up for me a crown of righteousness, which the Lord, the righteous judge, shall give me at that day: and not to me only, but unto all them also that love his appearing."—2 Timothy 4:7–8.

Paul never let up in his service for Christ until he crossed the finish line.

Simply dressing and talking like a golfer doesn't make one a golfer. In order to get into the game of golf, a person has to strike a golf ball with a club.

Likewise, dressing and talking like a Christian doesn't make one a Christian. In order to get into the game of life, a person must accept Christ as Lord and Savior.

Prop: Dress like a golfer. Have a bag of golf clubs and a golf ball. To illustrate the second point, I attach labels to several clubs, depicting one of them to represent each spiritual club. Project upon a screen a beautiful green and a fairway, complete with sand traps and perhaps water hazards.

12
No Dumping Allowed
Psalm 140:4

Have you ever seen a sign that reads *No Dumping Allowed*? People post such signs on their property trying to keep people from dumping unwanted trash. A *No Dumping Allowed* sign should be erected in your heart, demanding that evildoers not deposit ungodly stuff.

Say *No Dumping Allowed* to **cigarettes.** Cigarettes destroy health and kill. Boldly and persistently say to all who offer you a cigarette, "No dumping allowed. Don't dump your trash here."

Say *No Dumping Allowed* to **alcohol.** Beer and liquor kill the brain cells, damage every gland in the body, and may lead to a premature (early) death. Alcohol impairs judgment and leads to acts that otherwise would never be done. Say to all who encourage drinking, "No dumping allowed. I don't want that garbage in my life."

Say *No Dumping Allowed* to **drugs.** Drugs are substances like marijuana, cocaine, crack, and LSD which injure life. In being tempted to use drugs, regardless of name or form, shout loudly and clearly, "No dumping allowed."

Say *No Dumping Allowed* to **pornography.** Pornography is books, magazines, videos, websites, or movies that show people doing immoral things. If invited to look at such trash, say, "Don't dump your trash on me." Then immediately tell your parents of what they wanted you to do.

Say *No Dumping Allowed* to **slander.** Slander is unkind and untrue talk about a person which hurts people deeply.

Don't allow friends to share bad things about others with you. Tell them, "No dumping allowed."

Say *No Dumping Allowed* to **bad thoughts.** Friends may try to dump dirty thoughts into your mind. Don't let them. Dirty thoughts sow seeds of sexual misconduct. Today and for the rest of your life, say to such people, "No dumping allowed."

Make a decision to wear a *No Dumping Allowed* sign around your heart to all these things for the rest of your life.

Prop: Make a *No Dumping Allowed* sign to wear around your neck. While giving this talk, Velcro to this sign each item that one is to resist as it is discussed.

13
A Pretend-to-Be Christian
2 Corinthians 13:5

I am holding two apples. One of them is a fake. It is not real. Can you tell which one it is?

Did you know there are fake doctors? These are people who pretend to be doctors. They dress like doctors with stethoscopes hanging around their necks. They treat sick people like doctors and talk like doctors, but they are not real doctors.

There are fake flowers. We call them artificial flowers. These flowers look like real flowers, but they are not real flowers.

There are fake teeth. They look like real teeth and chew like real teeth, but they are false teeth. Have you ever seen someone with fake teeth?

The Bible says there are also fake Christians. These are people who look and talk like Christians, but they are just "pretend-to-be" Christians.

A pretend-to-be Christian might be **someone who is baptized.** Baptism doesn't make someone a Christian. A person is not baptized to become a Christian, but because he is a Christian.

Simon Magus was baptized, but he was not a Christian (Acts 8:13–23). There are a lot of children like him who think they are Christians because they have been baptized, but they are wrong. They are pretend-to-be Christians.

A pretend-to-be Christian might be **someone who attends church.** Many people think that because they go to church on Sunday, they are Christians, but they are mistaken. A man named Nicodemus attended church regularly, but he was not saved. Jesus told this man, "Ye must be born again" (John 3:7). Going to church cannot make a person a Christian any more than going to McDonald's can make a person a hamburger.

A pretend-to-be Christian may be **someone who does religious things.** Just because a person prays, witnesses, tithes, goes on mission trips, preaches, or sings gospel songs, that doesn't mean he is a Christian. What is done for Jesus doesn't make a person a Christian; rather, it is what Jesus does in them (Matthew 7:22–23). Christians do not do religious things in order to be saved, but because they are saved.

A pretend-to-be Christian can be **someone who lives a good life.** Keeping the Ten Commandments and living a clean life doesn't make a person a Christian. You can be good and still be lost. A person cannot earn salvation. People do not get to Heaven by the good things they do. A person's goodness doesn't count toward salvation. Be good and do good things, but never count on that to make you right with God.

A pretend-to-be Christian can be **someone who sincerely believes he is saved.** One can be a pretend-to-be Christian without knowing he is one. A person can really believe he is a Christian, when he actually is not. Such a person is sincere, but he is sincerely wrong.

How can you know if you are a pretend-to-be Christian or a real Christian? The Bible states:

"He that hath the Son hath life; and he that hath not the Son of God hath not life.
"These things have I written unto you that believe on the name of the Son of God; that ye may know that ye have

eternal life, and that ye may believe on the name of the Son of God."—I John 5:12–13.

A person who has repented of his sin (expressed sorrow for disobeying God's commandments and rejecting Jesus) and in faith (trust) asked Jesus into his life as Lord and Savior is a Christian. Don't be a pretend-to-be Christian. Be the real thing.

Prop: Two apples and two flowers—one each of which is fake. A set of play teeth that looks real.

14
Road Signs of Life
Proverbs 3:5–6

Along life's journey, there are several road signs that must be obeyed in order to arrive at your destination safely.

ONE WAY. This road sign is found in Matthew 7:13–14, in which Jesus said, "Enter through the narrow gate. The gate is wide and the road is wide that leads to Hell, and many people enter through that gate. But the gate is small and the road is narrow that leads to true life. Only a few people find that road" (NCV).

Jesus is the ONE road that leads to being right with God, having real life, and going to Heaven. If you have never before done so, say now, "I have decided to follow Jesus." Don't go Satan's way. It leads to utter heartache and Hell.

SPEED LIMIT. This road sign is found in Psalm 119, wherein David declared, "Blessed are they that keep His testimonies, and that seek Him with the whole heart....Thou hast commanded us to keep thy precepts diligently" (verses 2, 4). God's law is the moral code of conduct by which man is to live. Breaking God's law results in heartache and havoc in one's life.

YIELD. This spiritual road sign is found in Luke 9:23, in which Jesus emphatically said, "If people want to follow me, they must give up the things they want. They must be willing to give up their lives daily to follow me" (NCV). You must constantly practice self-denial, yielding to the will and way of God.

Practice daily death to the "Big I" (yourself), yielding to His control and ever praying, "Not my will, but yours, O

God, be done. Overrule my desires and plans, that your plan may be accomplished in and through me."

KEEP RIGHT. This spiritual road sign is found in Psalm 119:101. The psalmist says, "I have refrained my feet from every evil way, that I might keep thy word."

The best sermon is found on thousands of highway signs in America. It simply states, "Keep Right." Keep right. Though the stars fall from the sky, always do what is right, regardless of cost or consequence.

King Saul was told to destroy all the livestock of the Amalekites, but this he did not do. Upon being confronted with this failure to obey God, Saul tried to justify what he had done. Samuel told him frankly, "To obey is better than sacrifice, and to hearken than the fat of rams" (1 Samuel 15:22). He was telling King Saul that it is never right to do wrong in order to get a chance to do right.

Always remember that in life's journey. Always "Keep Right"!

EXIT—FOOD. This spiritual road sign can be found in 1 Peter 2:2: "Like newborn babies, you must crave pure spiritual milk so that you will grow into a full experience of salvation. Cry out for this nourishment" (NLT). As the body needs food to stay healthy, so the soul needs spiritual food to stay healthy. Daily feed on the Word of God in order to grow strong for Jesus.

HOSPITAL (BLUE H). This spiritual marker is found in Hebrews 10:25: "You should not stay away from the church meetings, as some are doing, but you should meet together and encourage each other. Do this even more as you see the day coming" (NCV). The church cares for the spiritually sick and hurting. It's a spiritual hospital of sorts. Everyone is in need of the "healing medicine" it offers—even you. Stay put in the church.

BUMP. This spiritual road sign is found in Romans 8:28: "And we know that God causes everything to work together for the good of those who love God and are called according to his purpose for them" (NLT). Christians are not exempt from trials, disappointments, and sorrow. Don't let them stagger your faith. God will be your holy shock absorber when such bumps are encountered.

NO DUMPING ALLOWED. This spiritual road sign is found in I Corinthians 15:33: "Do not be deceived: 'Bad company corrupts good morals'" (NASB). Don't let the ungodly dump the garbage of alcohol, drugs, or sex into your life. Select friends carefully. Choose as friends those who will be a spiritual challenge—an asset, not a deficit; a plus, not a minus in your life.

DO NOT ENTER. This spiritual marker is found in Proverbs 4:14: "Do not enter the path of the wicked, and do not walk in the way of the evil" (ESV). There are many "Do Not Enter" signs in the Bible that must be heeded, lest you get hurt. God knows certain places, people, and things will cause harm, so He puts this sign out in front of them for your protection.

STOP. This final spiritual road sign is found in I John 1:9: "If we confess our sins, he is faithful and just to forgive us our sins, and to cleanse us from all unrighteousness." It is at the moment of sin that you need to immediately STOP and ask Jesus for cleansing. Don't live with unconfessed and unforsaken sin! For Jesus, be as clean and pure as possible in your life, but when you do something that is bad (sin), stop immediately to ask Jesus' forgiveness before going any further.

I wish you God's best upon life's journey. Follow these road signs to a happy and meaningful life in Jesus Christ.

Prop: Use regular highway signs to illustrate each point, or have them made. Hold the appropriate sign before the children when it is being discussed.

15
God's Hand in the Glove of Your Life
John 15:4–8

The word *abide* means "to stay put." It is imperative that you abide, *stay put,* in Jesus, or else you will fizzle out spiritually.

There are two ways that one can make instant tea. The first is by dipping the tea bag in and out of the hot water. The second is by allowing the tea bag to remain (abide) in the hot water until it becomes totally saturated by the water.

Don't be a dipper spiritually, dipping in and out of fellowship with Christ; rather, be an abider, remaining steadfast, unmovable, always abounding in the things of God (1 Corinthians 15:58).

Envision a baseball glove lying on the ground. If a fly ball or grounder is hit right to the glove, could it make the catch? Obviously not. The glove cannot fulfill its purpose, unless a baseball player's hand is in the glove. Properly fitted on a hand that is abiding in it, that glove immediately becomes capable of anything the ballplayer can do.

Your life is like the glove. Apart from the hand of God inserted in your life, you accomplish nothing. However, with God's hand abiding in the glove of your life, you can do anything God designs.

And just as dirt in a finger of the glove prevents the ballplayer from having full control in its use, dirt in the believer's life hinders God's use of his life. Keep the glove clean and well-oiled for His use—24/7. You must "stay put" in Jesus to experience the victorious Christian life and the great and mighty things He will do through you.

Prop: Lay a softball glove on the floor and have a person roll a ball at it (couple of times).

Ask the children why the glove didn't catch the ball. They will respond that the glove has to be on your hand to catch the ball. Put the glove onto your hand and repeat the ball toss. This time the glove will catch the ball.

16
Tagging the Bases
1 John 5:11–13

The crack of Josh's bat resounded loudly through the stadium. The sports announcer shouted through the microphone, "It's a long fly ball into left field. Back, back, back goes the left fielder. That ball is out of here—home run!"

As Josh rounded the bases, the crowd of thousands on their feet cheered. As he tagged home plate, coaches and teammates gave him a big high five. Then he woke up. Ever had a dream like that? Bases in the game of baseball illustrate the Christian life.

First Base Stands for Salvation. How can you be saved? Three things explain this for us. First, understand that you have sinned (done wrong, disobeyed God) and that you are in need God's forgiveness. Second, understand that Jesus died upon a cross, was buried, and was raised from the dead to forgive sin, thus rescuing man from its consequence—separation from God now and forever. Finally, express sorrow for doing wrong, inviting Jesus into your life. It was June 9, 1972, at 9:15 p.m. when I tagged first base. Have you tagged it? If not, do so now.

Second Base Stands for Baptism and the Church. The years I played baseball were a great delight. It is almost as if I can still hear my coach saying, "That's it, Frank. First, tag first base; then get into second as fast as you can."

God is saying that to you. Tag first base in salvation; then quickly tag second base in baptism and church membership.

What is baptism? It pictures Jesus' death, burial and resurrection. It is a silent movie describing what happened to Jesus from Good Friday to Easter Morning. It preaches the Gospel.

Baptism states the same two things that my wedding band declares. My wedding band tells people I love Mary, my wife, and that I belong to her.

Baptism proclaims that we love Jesus and that we belong to Him. It does not save us, for only Jesus can do that. It is Jesus' command that everyone who loves Him be baptized.

Also at second base, slide into the church. Pray for the church, support the church, attend the church, give to the church, serve God in the church, and always be faithful to the church. The church is imperative for spiritual growth and obedience to God.

Third Base Stands for Service. I yet can hear my coach saying, "That's it, Frank; tag second base. Now get into third as fast as you can."

Our heavenly Coach is telling us to do the same. You ask, "But, Mr. Frank, what can I, as a child, do to serve God?"

Though not as exciting as serving God in Africa, you can render service by picking up trash from the church or school or park grounds, beautifying His creation. Anything done to help the needy is counted as service unto God, whether it is to those in the nursing home, in prison, at local shelters for the homeless, or the shut-in (Matthew 25:34–40). Visits, cards and care packages to those in need communicate God's love.

Further, we serve God in praying, giving of our allowance to the church, telling others of the story of Jesus, and standing up for what is right.

Home Plate Stands for Eternity. A tag at first base gives assurance that we will one day tag home plate in Heaven. I am looking forward to Heaven. "Heaven is a beautiful place, filled with glory and grace. I want to see my Savior's face. Heaven is a beautiful place. Want to go there!"

The only way we can go to the wonderful place of Heaven is by knowing Jesus as our Lord and Savior. If you haven't tagged first base, please think seriously about doing so now.

Prop: A baseball uniform, shoes, hat, glove, ball and bat, and a set of bases, including home plate. With the bases on the platform, invite the children to stand by the base they wish to tag in extending the invitation.

17

The Cross and Noah's Ark
Hebrews 11:7; Matt 27:27–35

The message of the cross is illustrated through Noah's Ark.

The cross is like Noah's Ark in its **purpose.** The purpose of Noah's Ark was to save people from the flood that was about to occur because of their sin. The purpose of the cross is to save people from the eternal separation from God which they deserve because of their sin. Boys and girls who come to Christ in faith and repentance will be saved from Hell, as those of Noah's day were saved from the flood.

The cross is like Noah's Ark in its **planning.** The Ark was not Noah's idea, but God's from beginning to end.

God not only told Noah to build it but how to build it— where the door was to be placed, where the window was to be set, and what kind of wood to use. God also instructed him as to its dimensions. It was to be 450 feet long, 45 feet tall and 75 feet wide. It would be one and a half times the size of a football field and shaped like a coffin.

The cross, like Noah's Ark, was entirely God's plan (1 Peter 1:18–20). The cross of Christ was no accident; it didn't just happen. It was all planned by God to make man's salvation possible.

The cross is like Noah's Ark in its **provision.** In the Ark, the needs of all were met by God for the 375 days they remained aboard. At Calvary, one discovers blood enough, pardon enough, power enough, grace enough, and mercy enough to meet every need. Jesus supplies all our need.

The cross is like Noah's Ark in its **protection.** The Ark protected and sheltered those within her walls from the judgment of God (the rain and the flood). Not a single drop of water touched any aboard the ark. Calvary protects all who are saved by Jesus' blood. The Christian never has to worry about going to Hell.

The cross is like Noah's Ark in its **invitation.** Noah was invited by God, not forced or commanded to enter the Ark. It would be Noah's decision entirely whether or not to enter. God invites (not forces) you to come to the cross to be saved. The decision is totally yours to do so or not to do so.

The cross is like Noah's Ark in it **entrance.** The Ark had only one door. The people and animals had to go through that door to gain entrance. There is but one door to salvation, and Jesus is that Door (John 10:9). A person has to enter this Door by repentance and faith if he is to be saved. There is no other way to become a Christian.

The cross is like Noah's Ark in its **control.** The Ark had no rudder or pilot's wheel, prohibiting its control by anyone but God. God and God alone dictated the movement of the Ark. In faith, Noah and his family members boarded the Ark and trusted God to guide and control their lives.

What a picture of faith! When we trust Jesus Christ as Lord and Savior, He takes control of our lives. There is no need to fear the future, for He is piloting the ship of our life.

The Cross is like Noah's Ark in its **preservation.** No one who entered the Ark died there. Christ has never lost a soul that has come to Him to be saved. He who is in Christ Jesus is as eternally secure as those in Heaven. Peter states that Christians are "kept by the power of God through faith unto salvation" (1 Peter 1:5). The saved will all arrive safely in Heaven.

The Cross is like Noah's Ark in its **opportunity.** A time came when the door of the Ark was shut and no one else could enter. The door to salvation in Jesus Christ has been open for 2,000 years, but, as in Noah's day, there will come a time when it will shut. No man knows when or how it will shut. The Door to salvation is presently open, so enter at once.

There weren't a bunch of arks in Noah's day that man could board to escape the flood. There was just one. There is just one way you may be saved, and that is through the cross of Jesus Christ. I invite you to receive Jesus into your life.

Prop: I had a type of Ark constructed for display, complete with a door of entrance. Each point in sequence was attached to the Ark. In conclusion, the children were invited to walk into the Ark.

18
The Gospel Armor
Ephesians 6:11–18

Armor is a special kind of suit worn for protection. Football players wear a type of armor for protection on the gridiron, and catchers wear it in the game of baseball. As a baseball catcher, my armor consisted of a chest protector, shin guards, mask, and, of course, a glove. This armor kept me from serious injury and kept me in the game. In the same way that athletes need armor for protection in athletic contests, Ephesians 6 states that Christians need spiritual armor for protection in the game of life.

The Belt of Truth speaks of the Christian's need to live that which he believes. It is important to read the Bible daily and seek to live out its teaching. The Bible shows what is right, what is not right, how to become right, and how to stay right.

The Breastplate of Righteousness speaks of the need to start each day clean and holy. The believer's first act of business each morning is to get himself right before God. He is not to carry any soiled laundry (sin) into a new day, but start it fresh and clean in heart.

The Gospel Shoes speak of the believer's assurance of salvation and witnessing passion. Wearing these shoes [full assurance of salvation] gives peace in difficult times and prompts sharing Christ with the lost.

The Shield of Faith speaks of the need to always believe God. Genesis 3 records how Satan lied to Eve. "'You won't die!' the serpent replied to the woman. God knows that your eyes will be opened as soon as you eat it, and you will be like God, knowing both good and evil. The woman was convinced. She saw that the tree was beautiful and its fruit looked delicious, and she wanted the wisdom it would give her. So she took some of the fruit and ate it" (verses 4–6, NLT). Eve believed Satan over God, the shield came down, and sin entered the world. Don't be like Eve; always believe God.

The Helmet of Salvation speaks of the need to look at the finish line in Heaven where Jesus awaits the saint's arrival. This helmet assures the believer that Heaven is his home. Additionally, the helmet protects the mind from being dominated by carnal and sensual thoughts.

The Sword of the Spirit speaks of the power of the Holy Scripture needed in our life. In the wilderness temptations, Jesus used the Sword of the Spirit (Scripture) to drive Satan back by declaring, "It is written..." (Matthew 4:1–11). "It is written" is like a dagger to Satan's heart. In temptation, quote Scripture to Satan, and he has to flee. Memorize Scripture to be ever ready for spiritual battle (Psalm 119:11).

How often should the gospel armor be worn? Daily. How is the gospel armor to be put on? Prayerfully. Paul instructs us, "Praying always with all prayer and supplication in the Spirit, and watching thereunto with all perseverance" (Ephesians 6:18). In daily clothing yourself with this spiritual armor, pray earnestly and continuously for God's protection, while being ever alert to the ambushes of Satan.

Prop: A catcher and football player's armor. Actual armor as described in Ephesians 6. As you proceed with the talk, dress an assistant in the armor point by point. Four arrows, each attached to a posterboard strip bearing one of the following words: "despair," "discouragement," "doubt," or "lust."

19
What Can You Do with Jesus?
Matthew 27:22

Imagine driving the car of your life down life's highway when all of a sudden you see Jesus standing on the side of the road wanting a ride.[10] What can you do with Jesus in such a case?

You can keep going, refusing Him entrance into your life. Sadly, many people pass Jesus by without considering who He is and what He did for them on the cross. Don't be like them.

You can offer Jesus a ride in the trunk of the car of your life. In the trunk of a car, out of sight, is a spare tire, just in case a tire on the car goes flat. A lot of people put Jesus in the trunk of their life (out of sight) for times of trouble. Jesus wants to help in times of trouble, but He both desires and deserves to have a greater role.

You can offer Jesus a ride in the back seat of the car of your life. Sometimes placards (small signs) that read, "No back seat drivers allowed" are placed in cars. The people driving these cars do not want anyone telling them how to drive. Many Christians have put Jesus in the back seat of their lives facing such a placard ("No back seat drivers allowed"). Such Christians refuse to allow Jesus to tell them how to drive the car of life concerning friends, entertainment, parents, and lifework.

You can offer Jesus a ride in the front seat passenger side. You can invite Jesus to sit in the front passenger seat. This option is far better than the others discussed, but it is still not the best, because you still are sitting in the place of control (behind the steering wheel).

You can invite Jesus to drive the car. You can hand Jesus the key to the car of your life, allowing Him to take control completely. This is the best decision that can be made concerning Jesus Christ. With His hands on the steering wheel and His feet on the accelerator and brakes, you will have a safe and wonderful journey to Heaven.

This illustration explains what the Bible states are your options concerning Jesus. What will you do with Jesus? Will you leave Him outside your life? Will you put Him in the trunk? Will He be in the back seat or on the front seat passenger side? Or will you allow Him to become your Lord and Savior?

Prop: A child's large toy car, a ring of keys, and a cross. Use the cross as symbol for Jesus on the side of the road hitchhiking, and the car as a symbol of everybody's life.

20
The Key to Heaven
John 10:9

A key is used to give entrance to a place that we want to enter. The Bible makes it clear that there is but one key to Heaven's Door. The key is not a literal key, but a spiritual one. What do you think this one key to Heaven is?

Is it the **Key of a Good Life?** Some people believe that if they live a good, clean life, they will go to Heaven. Let's see if this key of a good life will open the door to Heaven? Do you believe it will? Here goes. You are right. It will not open Heaven's door.

Is it the **Key of Baptism?** A lot of children think that baptism will take them to Heaven. Are they right? Do you believe the key of baptism will open Heaven's door? Let's see. You are right; it will not. A person is baptized because he is a Christian, not in order to become a Christian.

Is it the **Key of Churchgoing?** Do you think a person goes to be with God in Heaven because he or she attended church? Is this the Key we are looking for to open Heaven's Door? Let's try it. No, it isn't. Jesus wants you to attend services and help the church, but always remember that doing so will not get you to Heaven.

Is it the **Key of a Christian Home?** Do you think that a child reared in a home where the Bible is read and prayer is made will go to Heaven? Is this the key to Heaven's door? Let's see if this key of a Christian home will open Heaven's door. Do you believe it will? Here goes. No it cannot. Thank God for a Christian home, but never trust it to take you to Heaven.

Is it the **Key of Religious Works?** Some think they can earn their way to Heaven by doing stuff for God like feeding the hungry, helping the poor, and teaching or singing about Jesus. Are they right? Will the key of doing good things for God open Heaven's Door? How many of you believe that it will? No, it cannot. Jesus states that doing a lot of wonderful things for God and others doesn't mean that the person doing the works will go to Heaven (Matthew 7:21–23).

Is it the **Key of the Lord's Supper?** The elements in the Lord's Supper—the bread and the juice—remind us of what Jesus did on the cross. Do you think that eating the bread and drinking the juice is the key to Heaven's door? How many of you believe this key of the Lord's Supper will open the door to Heaven? Let's try it and see. It will not. The Lord's Supper simply remind us of the price Jesus paid for our salvation.

There is one final key to consider. It is the **Key Jesus Christ.** He said, "I am the way, the truth, and the life *(the key)*: no man cometh unto the Father *(Heaven),* but by me" (John 14:6). How many of you believe Jesus is the key to Heaven's door? Let's see if you are right. You are correct, for Jesus opens the door to Heaven for all who trust Him. The only way to be right with God and go to Heaven is by giving your life to Jesus Christ.

Prop: A framed structure that looks like a house, complete with a door and a working door lock. Inscribe over the top of the door "HEAVEN." Get six keys that don't fit the lock and one that does. Upon completing each point, try a nonworking key in the lock, illustrating that it will not open the door to Heaven. When you share the key of Jesus, insert the correct key into the door, indicating that He alone can open the door to Heaven.

21
The Knocking Savior
Revelation 3:20

Holman Hunt painted a picture entitled *The Light of the World* in which he depicts Jesus with a lamp in His hand knocking on a door. The door is latched from the inside, and no one opens it. The painting is based upon Revelation 3:20.

Who is the **Knocking Person?** Who is He that is knocking on your heart's door seeking entrance? Holman Hunt is exactly correct in describing Him as Jesus Christ. Jesus is God's only Son, who died upon a cross and rose from the dead to make possible the salvation of the world.

What is the **Knocking Purpose?** Why does Jesus knock upon your heart's door? It is to gain entrance into your life so you may be the recipient of His free gift of salvation. Jesus wants to give you what is needed to live life abundantly and eternally with Him.

Where is the **Knocking Place?** Where does Jesus knock seeking entrance? Our text states that He knocks at our heart's door. This pictures Jesus as very close to us, for you cannot be very far away from a door and still knock upon it.

There are several door knockers which Jesus may use to knock on the door of a person's heart to gain entrance. He uses *church services.* It was in a church service that I heard His knock on my heart's door and let Him enter. He uses *preachers and Bible teachers.* God may knock on your heart's door through a Sunday school teacher, children's worker or pastor, so always stay alert to what they share. He uses *friends* to knock on our heart's door. Often God will prompt a friend to urge us to stop doing something wrong, start doing something right, or receive Jesus into our life as Lord and Savior. He knocks on our heart's door through *the Bible*. Did you know that people have been saved simply by reading the Bible? It is a powerful door knocker. The Bible is God's love letter giving instruction as to how to live. Read and listen for God's knocking through its pages. God also knocks on our heart's door through the *conscience*. The conscience tells a person it is wrong to do certain things and right to do others. It tells us it is wrong to disobey God. If we listen closely to our conscience, it will tell of our need to receive Jesus into our life as Lord and Savior. The conscience is one of God's biggest door knockers seeking entrance into our life.

What is the **Knocking Promise?** Jesus promises to enter into the life of every person who opens his or her heart's door to Him ("I will come in."). Sincerely invite Jesus into your heart to be your Lord and Savior, and He will enter. God keeps His promises; He cannot lie (Hebrews 6:18). Is Jesus knocking on your heart's door seeking entrance? Open the door through faith and repentance (Acts 20:21), and He certainly will enter.

Prop: A sheet of plywood painted red and cut out into the shape of a heart. In the center of the heart, fasten a door knocker. Make poster strips to represent each door knocker (services, preachers, friends, Bible, conscience) to fasten onto this heart as it is shared in the talk. Attach the name of the door knocker to the heart with Velcro; it makes a loud noise as you illustrate the point.

22

The Lord's Supper
1 Corinthians 11:23–30

The church observes the Lord's Supper using small cups of grape juice and small wafers. The Lord's Supper pictures salvation.

It pictures Christ. "This do in remembrance of me" (verse 24). The Lord's Supper is all about Jesus' death on Calvary. When we come to this table, Jesus wants us to think about the death He died upon the Cross.

It pictures Calvary. It not only pictures that He died, but also how He died. He died willingly and lovingly. Jesus wants us to remember the crown of jagged thorns pressed upon His head, the spear that pierced His side, the nails hammered into His feet and hands, and the blood He shed for you and me.

It pictures Celebration. The Lord's Supper is a celebration party concerning that all Christ did at Calvary. Everything it says speaks of joy and hope. Matthew's account of the Lord's Supper states that this celebration included singing. In coming to this table, celebrate Jesus and what He did which no other one could do.

It pictures Communion. The disciples at the Last Supper with Jesus sat at one table, joined in one meal, ate of one loaf, and drank of one cup. It pictured their oneness with each other and with Christ. Jesus wants us to have that same kind of fellowship with Him and others.

It pictures Commission (service God wants believers to do). The Lord's Supper is a visible sermon of the message and meaning of the Cross. To those who do not love Jesus, it is a testimony of God's awesome love for them. All this Supper teaches, believers are to proclaim to the world.

It pictures Consummation. That's a big word. It simply means one day Jesus will come back to take those who love Him to Heaven. "Till he come" (verse 26)—this is a promise Jesus will keep. That's going to be a wonderful day.

It pictures Confession. Who is to partake of the Lord's Supper? The Lord's Supper is only for those who know Jesus Christ as Lord and Savior. It is important that all sin be confessed and forgiven before partaking of this observance. The next time your church observes the Lord's Supper, remember these things that it pictures and thank Jesus for all He did to make salvation possible.

Prop: Lord's Supper elements and pictures of each point in the talk for further clarity.

23
Unsafe Lifeboats
Acts 27:27–33

The apostle Paul was traveling by ship to Rome when a fierce storm developed that caused the ship to sink. Sailors, in an effort to escape, lowered a lifeboat into the water. Seeing this, Paul cried to the centurion and to the soldiers, "Except these abide in the ship, ye cannot be saved" (verse 31). The sailors immediately cut the rope from the lifeboat, allowing it to drift away. All aboard were later saved.

Man has shipwrecked his life (Ship of Life), and Satan seeks to get him to board several unsafe lifeboats in an attempt to escape.

The Unsafe Lifeboat of a Good Life. Often, people want to jump into this lifeboat, thinking that a good life will take them to Heaven—but it cannot. I'm all for living as clean and pure a life as one possibly can, but no one goes to Heaven because he or she does so. The Scripture states, "But we are all as an unclean thing, and all our righteousnesses are as filthy rags" (Isaiah 64:6).

Cut this lifeboat loose, because it certainly will sink long before it reaches Heaven's shore. Don't get on this lifeboat.

The Unsafe Lifeboat of Baptism. Thousands think that the lifeboat of baptism will take them to Heaven, but are they right? A person is saved from sin by believing in Jesus, not by being baptized. How many people did Jesus baptize? John 4:2 tells us: "Jesus himself baptized not, but his disciples." That's right—zero! He didn't baptize a single person. If baptism saves, then that means Jesus didn't save anyone. But it doesn't save, and Jesus has saved millions of people throughout history.

Cut this lifeboat loose, for it will not get you to Heaven.

The Unsafe Lifeboat of Church Attendance. Simply going to church will not make you a Christian. Go to church, support the church, pray for the church, give to the church, worship God in church, and serve God through the church; but never look to the church to save you. Going to church and being a Christian go together, but they are not the same. Christians should go to church, but not everyone who goes to church is a Christian.

This lifeboat of trust in the church to get us to Heaven will sink. Cut it loose.

The Unsafe Lifeboat of a Christian Family. Some believe that they are going to Heaven because of being reared in a Christian home. Being born in a Christian home will not make you a Christian any more than being born at McDonald's would make you a hamburger. Thank God for Christian parents, but never trust their salvation to get you to Heaven. Put your trust in Christ personally.

Let's cut this unsafe lifeboat loose, for it will not get us to Heaven.

The Unsafe Lifeboat of the Lord's Supper. The Lord's Supper reminds us of what Jesus did on the Cross. The juice pictures His shed blood to forgive sin, and the bread symbolizes His broken body. Simply drinking the juice and eating the bread does not save one from sin. The Lord's Supper has no power to cleanse from sin.

Cut the rope to this lifeboat, for it is certainly unsafe and will not get you to Heaven.

The Unsafe Lifeboat of Good Works. There is no way to work your way to Heaven, to merit God's favor. Do good deeds as much as possible, but never count on them to take you to Heaven. One can be a preacher, missionary, soul winner, singer, tither, or social worker, but if he doesn't have a personal relationship with Jesus Christ, he will not go to Heaven. Don't depend on what *you* do to take you to Heaven, but upon what *He* did on the Cross.

Let's cut this unsafe lifeboat loose, for it will not get us safely to Heaven.

The Safe Lifeboat That Goes to Heaven. What then is the lifeboat that God has provided to rescue man from the Ocean of Sin and grant him safe travel to Heaven? This lifeboat is made out of the very tree that stood on a hill called Calvary two thousand years ago. It has been carrying passengers to Heaven for all this time without losing a single person.

The lifeboat is Jesus Christ, God's only Son, who died and was raised from the dead to make salvation possible. I'm glad that I'm aboard that lifeboat, and I invite you to join me.

You ask, "Mr. Frank, how can I get on this lifeboat to Heaven?" You do so by 'repentance and faith' (Acts 20:21). First, realize that you have sinned against God by failure to keep the Ten Commandments. Express sorrow to God for these acts of disobedience, telling Him you no longer want to live as you have in the past. Second, by faith, receive Jesus into your life as Lord and Savior.

Prop: Draw seven lifeboats upon water on separate pieces of large posterboard. Below each lifeboat, write its name; for example, "The Unsafe Lifeboat of Baptism." Make a hole in the posterboard on its right side center, through which a thin rope should be inserted and tied off.

An assistant should hold the posterboard of the lifeboat being discussed. At the conclusion of each lifeboat point, hold the loose end of the rope, take scissors, and cut it loose. For the final lifeboat, name it Jesus and draw it in the shape of a Cross.

24
Keep a Tight Grip
2 Samuel 23:9–10

Eleazar was a champion for God. He fought so valiantly and courageously that at battle's end he could not lay his sword down, because its hilt had become imbedded in his hand. That's standing for God isn't it? As Eleazar kept a tight grip upon his sword, I challenge you to be a champion for God by keeping a tight grip on several very important things.

Keep a tight grip on **your Parents.** A prophecy fulfilled in our day is Matthew 10:21, which states, "And the children shall rise up against their parents, and cause them to be put to death." Many children are rising up against their parents through disobedience and disrespect. Don't join them; keep honoring your parents in attitude and action. You owe them nothing short of utmost respect, love, and gratitude.

Keep a tight grip on **the People of God.** Friends are either firefighters or firestarters. Firefighters try to extinguish the flame of Jesus in a person's life, while the firestarters enable the fire to burn hotter. Keep tight grips on friends who are firestarters, and avoid the firefighters. With David, say, "I am a companion of all them that fear thee [God], and of them that keep thy precepts" (Psalm 119:63).

Keep a tight grip on **the Plan of God.** God has a wonderful plan regarding a life's work (career, job) for you when you get older. The plan may be to be a pastor, missionary, evangelist, musician, or chaplain. Many missionaries testify that it was when they were children that God called them into missionary service. Stay alert and open to God's call, ever listening for it. Should God call you into full-time

Christian service, say joyfully as Isaiah, "Here am I; send me" (Isaiah 6:8), and keep a tight grip on that call all of your life.

Keep a tight grip on **the Precious Word of God.** The Bible is the Word of God, who cannot lie. Believe it against the opinion of any friend, teacher, or minister. Love the Bible, learn the Bible, and live the Bible. Say, and mean, "The B-i-b-l-e, yes, that's the Book for me. I stand alone on the Word of God, the B-i-b-l-e."

Keep a tight grip on **your Purity.** Don't let anyone talk you into doing something which is impure (morally unclean). Always do what is right. Do right, though the stars fall from the sky. It's never right to do wrong. Never drink alcohol, smoke cigarettes, use drugs, look at pornography, or do anything sexually wrong. Determine to be a champion for God, as Eleazar was, by keeping a tight grip on each of these things.

Prop: A large sword to which each talking point is attached. Plastic swords about 3 or 4 inches long may be distributed at the end of the talk as a reminder of the lesson. (A bulk bag of plastic swords is inexpensive. Purchase the type with blunted ends.)

25
Who Are Christians?
Acts 11:26

As a child, I recall completing a form in Sunday school that asked, "Are you a Christian?" I was clueless as to what that meant. Perhaps you are as well.

Who are Christians?

Christians are **Saved People.** "Saved" is a good Bible word. Luke tells us that Jesus came into this world to seek and save those that are lost (Luke 19:10).

In the church, Christians sing, "We have heard the joyful sound: Jesus saves; Jesus saves"; and, "Amazing grace, how sweet the sound that saved a wretch like me."

The word "saved" means to be rescued from all that is wrapped up in the words sin, Satan, and Hell, unto a wonderful life with Jesus forever. Jesus invites all to be saved: "Come unto me" (Matthew 11:28). And the coming to Jesus that saves is a simple reliance (trust) in Him.

Christians are **Secure People.** Once Jesus gets you, Satan can never have you. Once a person is saved, he always will be saved (John 10:29). God holds His children in the palm of His hand, clutching them tightly.

What would happen if I hit an egg with a hammer? It would crack and splash everywhere. However, if the egg were placed under a metal pot and then struck, it would be unharmed.

Christians are like the egg, Satan is like the hammer, and Jesus is like the pot. At the moment of salvation, Jesus covers the saved person with His protection from the power of Satan. The Christian is safe and secure in the arms of Jesus.

Christians are **Singing People.** God gives birth to a song in the life of the saved. Christians sing songs that the lost do not (Revelation 5:9).

It's a song of joy. "Happy day, happy day, when Jesus washed my sins away. He taught me how to watch and pray and live rejoicing every day. Happy day, happy day, when Jesus washed my sins away."

It's a song of peace. "I have peace like a river; I have peace like a river. I have peace like river in my soul."

It's a song of praise. "Thank you, Lord, for saving my soul. Thank you, Lord, for making me whole. Thank you, Lord, for giving to me Thy great salvation so rich and free."

It's a song of hope. "When Christ shall come with shout of acclamation to take me home, what joy shall fill my heart! Then I shall bow in humble adoration and there proclaim, my God, how great Thou art!"

If you don't have a spiritual song, you don't have a Savior.

Christians are **Satisfied People.** A Christian is a joyous person whose every need is supplied through Jesus. Jesus satisfies the soul like wealth, fame, popularity, friends, alcohol, drugs, or pleasure cannot.

A song states: "There's a hole in my heart that cannot be filled with the things that I do. There's a hole in my heart that can only be filled with You. Wholehearted; wholehearted!"

There is a hole in our hearts that cannot be filled with anything or anyone but Jesus Christ, and when He fills it, life takes on new meaning and happiness.

Christians are **Separated People.** A Christian lives differently from those who do not love Jesus (2 Corinthians 6:17).

When Queen Mary and Elizabeth were little girls, they stopped for water while riding their horses in the woods. When they were leaving, the lady who served them the water said, "There's something special about you girls. You are so ladylike."

The girls answered, "There's nothing special about us, but there is something special about our father. He is the King of England."

People ought to say "There's something special about you. You are so different in how you talk and live." Christians, as children of the King, live differently from the lost world.

Christians are **Sharing People.** David said, "Let the redeemed of the LORD say so, whom he hath redeemed from the hand of the enemy" (Psalm 107:2). Christians tell other people about Jesus. Who can you tell today about Jesus?

Who are Christians? They are saved people, secure people, singing people, satisfied people, separated people, and sharing people. Are you a Christian?

Prop: Using a large piece of Styrofoam, cut out a figure of a person and write across the chest "Christian." Pin each descriptive point of a Christian on this cutout as the talk is shared.

This same approach may be used with a real person, except you should hang a sign around his neck that reads "Christian" and then let him attach the descriptive points of a Christian to himself as the talk is given.

26
The Ten Commandments
Exodus 20:3–17

The Ten Commandments (rules) teach what God expects of our lives, how we should treat God and others. Each commandment is for you and me personally. God, in saying, "Thou shalt not," is saying, "You should not." Here are the Ten Commandments from the English Standard Version.

Rule One Is Love God More Than Anything. "You shall have no other gods before me." Put God ahead of sports, play, heroes, friends, and family. Obedience to this first commandment enables the keeping of the other nine.

Rule Two Is Worship God Rightly. "You shall not make for yourself a carved image." The first rule gives instruction as to whom to worship; this one tells us how to worship.

Did you know that some people worship crosses, statues and pictures of God? This rule tells the Christian such worship is wrong. People are to worship God personally, not a representation of God.

Rule Three Is Don't Misuse God's Name. "You shall not take the name of the LORD your God in vain." Don't use God's name in a wrong way through cursing, slang or in jokes that belittle Him. Use your tongue to honor, not demean, (belittle) God.

Rule Four Is Remember the Lord's Day. "Remember the Sabbath day, to keep it holy."

The Chinese have a legend about a man who went into a village with a string of seven coins. In compassion, he gave six of these coins to a beggar. He placed the last coin in his pocket. The beggar happened to be a thief, who then stole the man's last coin.

This is what many have done with Sunday. God has given man six days to work and play, yet he has taken for his own use God's day designed for worship and rest.

What can we do to make Sunday special to us and to God? We can attend church, spend more time with God in Bible study and prayer, rest, and help others.

Rule Five Is Honor Your Parents. "Honor your father and your mother." Honor means "to prize highly, show respect, and treat as precious or valuable." God instructs us to treat our parents with the highest respect possible and to prize them above all else.

A chief way children honor their parents is with the demonstration (showing) of love and obedience. Always come when they call quickly; do what they say without argument and do so happily; never raise your voice to them.

Rule Six Is Do Not Murder. "You shall not murder." Every person's life is precious to God, whether it be an unborn baby's life, a stranger's life, the life of friends or your own life. It is always wrong to commit murder. Don't try to get even with someone who brings harm to you.

Rule Seven Is Keep Yourself Pure. "You shall not commit adultery." This is God's rule about marriage.

Adam and Eve were the first couple to get married, a marriage God designed to last. God expects the same of every marriage. Stay pure and clean in mind and body.

Rule Eight Is You Shall Not Steal. "You shall not steal." Stealing is taking something that doesn't belong to you, whether it is a piece of bubble gum or a bicycle.

The value or size of what one takes doesn't make it any more or less of a theft. Cheating in games is a form of stealing. Cheating on school tests is a form of stealing. And God says, "You shall not steal."

Rule Nine Is Don't Lie. "You shall not bear false witness." Tell the truth.

In Ephesians 4:25, the apostle Paul gives instruction to put away lying. What is a lie? It is speaking untruth about someone or something.

Do you remember the fairy tale of Pinocchio? Pinocchio's noise grew longer with each lie he told. What if that happened to your nose with each lie you told?

Always speak the truth, even if it means being punished.

Rule Ten Is You Shall Not Covet. "You shall not covet."

Be content and happy with your attraction and possessions. Don't murmur or complain, but be thankful for who you are and what God has given to you.

Have you always obeyed all the commandments? Indeed not, for no one has obeyed them without failure. Only Jesus can help you to keep them.

Prop: Using large pieces of Styrofoam, cut out two "tablets of stone." On each, attach small hangers on which commandments (written on poster paper) may be hung as they are discussed in the talk.

27
Ten Commandments and Ten Fingers
Exodus 20:3–17

I want to use our ten fingers to explain the Ten Commandments.[11]

Hold up the index finger of the right hand to show that God is to be number One in your life.

Hold up the second finger to show that there are not two gods; there is only one.

Hold up the third finger with the first two to form the letter *W* and show the need to watch our words.

Hold up four fingers with your thumb resting under them to show that Sunday is a day to rest.

Hold up five fingers like making a pledge to honor your parents.

Hold up the index finger of the left hand, and use it as a gun shooting at the other hand to show that we shouldn't hurt others.

Hold out one hand flat and pretend it is a church floor. Place two fingers on this floor to show the need for a husband and a wife to be true to each other and keep their marriage vows.

Slightly press the four fingers of each hand together, forming a prison cell to show what happens if one steals.

Hold up five fingers on one hand and four on the other. Fold the thumb under the four fingers like it is hiding, and turn your hand around. The thumb is telling the four fingers on that hand hurtful things and lies about the five fingers on the other hand. The thumb is lying, and God tells us not to lie.

Hold out both hands, palms up, and wiggle each finger to show you have the "gimmies." They are saying, "I want what's yours, so give it to me." God wants us to be content and happy with what He chooses to give us.

Prop: Your hands.

28
David and Goliath
1 Samuel 17

The giant Goliath wanted a soldier from King Saul's army with whom to fight. The winner of that duel would determine whether the Philistines or the Israelites would be declared the victor of the day.

However, no soldier wanted to fight Goliath, who stood over nine feet tall and wore heavy battle armor. That is, not until a young man named David arrived, willing to do what the experienced soldiers in Saul's army were afraid to do.

In facing the big challenge, David refused to let others discourage or stop him. He was determined from the get-go to do what God wanted.

How can we do the big things that God wants us do?[12]

Think Big. David asked the soldiers, "What shall be done to the man that killeth this Philistine, and taketh away the reproach from Israel? for who is this uncircumcised Philistine, that he should defy the armies of the living God?" (verse 26). David thought big long before he ever did big.

Think Big about the big things God wants you to do. Don't allow anyone talk you out of doing what God puts in your heart to accomplish. In verses 28 and 29, we see that David's oldest brother was angry with him and accused him of having a bad motive for being there, but David would not let that stop him from doing what needed to be done for God.

Has God put in your heart the desire to be a missionary, a pastor, an evangelist, a musician, or a politician? If so, keep

89

thinking big about doing it, even though it seems a long way off or impossible.

Talk Big. David told King Saul, "Thy servant slew both the lion and the bear: and this uncircumcised Philistine shall be as one of them, seeing he hath defied the armies of the living God....The LORD that delivered me out of the paw of the lion, and out of the paw of the bear, he will deliver me out of the hand of this Philistine" (verses 36–37).

David spoke some "big talk," assuring the King that because God was with him, he would defeat Goliath. The gist of what David was telling the King was this: "It's in the bag. It's a done deal. I am going to defeat him, because God is with me."

That's a "faith" kind of talking. Don't be afraid to talk big about God's assignment. Though he was ridiculed (Genesis 37:19), Joseph remained unstoppable in talking big about what God wanted him to do.

You may be ridiculed like Joseph was, possibly even by family members, but, like Joseph, refuse to quit doing what God wants you to do.

Believe Big. David not only thought big and talked big; he also believed big. In facing Goliath he declared, "Thou comest to me with a sword, and with a spear, and with a shield: but I come to thee in the name of the LORD of hosts, the God of the armies of Israel, whom thou hast defied. This day will the LORD deliver thee into mine hand; and I will smite thee, and take thine head from thee" (verses 45–46).

David was confident that God would enable him to defeat Goliath. Think big and talk big, but believe big. Regardless of the bigness of the task, never doubt that God will help you to do it. Believing big is what the Bible calls faith (Hebrews 11:6).

Do Big. Thinking big, talking big, and believing big are nothing, unless one *does* big. David did big.

"And it came to pass, when the Philistine arose, and came and drew nigh to meet David, that David hasted, and ran toward the army to meet the Philistine.

"And David put his hand in his bag, and took thence a stone, and slang it, and smote the Philistine in his forehead, that the stone sunk into his forehead; and he fell upon his face to the earth.

"So David prevailed over the Philistine with a sling and with a stone, and smote the Philistine, and slew him; but there was no sword in the hand of David."—verses 48–50.

David did what God put in his heart to do. Think big about what God wants you to do, talk big about it, believe big about it, but then do big about it.

There are many who think big, talk big, and believe big who never do big. Use this time in your life to prepare for that time later in life when you will have the opportunity to do big things for God.

Many missionaries testify that it was while they were children that God put in their heart the desire to be missionaries. Missionary service, as with any other ministry, begins with thinking big, talking big, and believing big. Only then can one do big.

Keep listening to God about what He wants you to do, and never doubt that He is able to bring it to pass (Philippians 1:6).

Prop: A large drawing of Goliath and a slingshot. The slingshot represents David as he fights Goliath. As you speak, dramatize each talking point that leads to David's doing big.

29
Five Things to Remember
Psalm 105:5

Thread tied to a finger or fingers serves to remind a person of something. Envision thread tied to each of my fingers as a reminder of five things God wants Christians to remember.

The thread on my thumb is so I will remember the message of **Christmas.** "And she brought forth her firstborn son, and wrapped him in swaddling clothes, and laid him in a manger; because there was no room for them in the inn" (Luke 2:7).

God gave the first Christmas gift, that of His only Son, Jesus, who was born in Bethlehem's manger and later died upon the cross to make man's salvation possible. What kind of gift can you give Jesus?

Take a Christmas bow, place it on your heart, and give yourself to Him. You can give Jesus no greater gift than that of yourself.

The thread on my index finger is to remind me of the message of **Good Friday** (Matthew 27:26–37). Never forget the suffering and pain Jesus experienced before and upon the cross—the whip that slashed His precious back, the crown of jagged thorns pressed upon His brow, the nails hammered into His feet and hands, the sword that pierced His side, and the soldiers who played at the foot of His cross while others made fun of Him.

In response to the bad things which the soldiers did to Him, remember that He said, "Father, forgive them; for they know not what they do" (Luke 23:34). Jesus did all this out of love that we might be saved. "For God so loved the world, that he gave his only begotten Son, that whosoever believeth in him should not perish, but have everlasting life" (John 3:16).

The thread on my tallest finger is a reminder of the message of **Easter.**

"In the end of the sabbath, as it began to dawn toward the first day of the week, came Mary Magdalene and the other Mary to see the sepulchre.

"And, behold, there was a great earthquake: for the angel of the Lord descended from heaven, and came and rolled back the stone from the door, and sat upon it.

"His countenance was like lightning, and his raiment white as snow:

"And for fear of him the keepers did shake, and became as dead men.

"And the angel answered and said unto the women, Fear not ye: for I know that ye seek Jesus, which was crucified.

"He is not here: for he is risen, as he said. Come, see the place where the Lord lay.

"And go quickly, and tell his disciples that he is risen from the dead; and, behold, he goeth before you into Galilee; there shall ye see him: lo, I have told you."—Matthew 28:1–7.

Roman soldiers guarded Jesus' tomb to make sure nobody would steal His body and pretend that He had risen from the dead. But what happened on Easter morning? He was raised from the dead. Jesus is alive and lives forevermore.

The thread on my ring finger is so I won't forget the message of the **Ascension.**

"And when he had spoken these things, while they beheld, he was taken up; and a cloud received him out of their sight.

Five Things to Remember

"And while they looked stedfastly toward heaven as he went up, behold, two men stood by them in white apparel;

"Which also said, Ye men of Galilee, why stand ye gazing up into heaven? this same Jesus, which is taken up from you into heaven, shall so come in like manner as ye have seen him go into heaven."—Acts 1:9–11.

Have you ever tried to cover up your footprints on the beach or tried to follow the footprints of another? In a way, we are following the footprints of Jesus in this sermon. We saw them first on the ground in Bethlehem, followed them to the Cross, then to the empty tomb, and now to the mount of ascension where Jesus was taken up to Heaven to get things ready for our arrival.

The thread on my smallest finger is to remind me of the message of the Second Coming.

"For the Lord himself shall descend from heaven with a shout, with the voice of the archangel, and with the trump of God: and the dead in Christ shall rise first:

"Then we which are alive and remain shall be caught up together with them in the clouds, to meet the Lord in the air: and so shall we ever be with the Lord.

"Wherefore comfort one another with these words."— 1 Thessalonians 4:16–18.

Jesus promises to return to take believers to Heaven. No one knows the day or hour of His return.

In Heaven, there will be no more sin, separation, sorrow, or suffering. Heaven is a place of perfect peace and joy.

Jesus possibly may return today. Never forget that Jesus promised to come back to take His children to Heaven, a promise He will keep. Have you repented of your sin (told God you were sorry for doing wrong) and in faith (trust) received Jesus into your life as Lord and Savior (Acts 20:21)?

Prop: Thread tied to each of five fingers. A large posterboard and cutouts of footprints, each labeled with the main talking points.

30
God's Umbrellas
Psalm 3:3

Umbrellas have been around for hundreds of years and are used to protect people from the sun, rain, and sometimes snow. The Bible talks about four kinds of spiritual "umbrellas" God gives Christians for protection.

First, there is the umbrella of **Salvation.** This umbrella protects the Christian's relationship with Jesus. It assures us that Satan cannot steal or destroy it. Once one is a child of God, he is always a child of God. Salvation protects us from Hell (Satan cannot keep a Christian out of Heaven) and from fear that God will abandon us (Jesus promises in Hebrews 13:5 that He will never leave us nor forsake us).

A second kind of umbrella God gives His children is **Christian Friends.** Friends love through all kinds of weather (Proverbs 17:17). God gives Christian friends to protect and help us in life. To David, God gave Jonathan; to Timothy, He gave Paul; to John Mark, He gave Barnabas. Whom has He given you?

You are not expected to live the Christian life alone. Have you heard the saying, "I've got your back?" God has given you friends who've "got your back," friends whom He has put in your life to help you face trouble and to give you encouragement. God also gives parents to protect you from bad things, so it is important to do what they say (to stay under their umbrella of protection).

The third kind of umbrella God gives believers is the **Bible.** It protects from sin. David said, "Thy word have I hid in mine heart, that I might not sin against thee" (Psalm 119:11).

The Bible protects us from untruth. Satan wants us to believe lies about God and himself, but the Bible is our protector from such attacks. It also protects us from harm. Obeying the Bible keeps a lot of bad things from happening to us.

Another type of umbrella God has given us is the **Holy Spirit.** The Holy Spirit is the third person of the Trinity who lives in Christians. He will protect and keep us safe from misunderstanding the teachings in the Bible, making wrong decisions, and missing God's plan for life. The Holy Spirit also protects us from unbearable sorrow when someone dies or is badly sick. The Bible says the Holy Spirit is our Comforter and Helper in time of need (John 14:16).

But as with any umbrella, God's umbrellas must be used if they are to protect us. An umbrella will do me no good in a rainstorm if it is unopened. The same is true with regard to God's umbrellas of protection.

When you open an umbrella, it shields you from the rain. Stand outside the open umbrella, and you will get drenched. As long as you remain under the umbrellas of God's protection, you'll be shielded from a lot of bad stuff. If you step out from under that protective cover, however, you will be hurt. Are you under the umbrella of God's salvation? Have you invited Jesus into your heart as Lord and Savior?

Prop: Four umbrellas, each with a posterboard attachment inscribed with one of the talking points. Umbrellas should be open on the platform for ease in transitioning from one point to the next. Actually, hold each umbrella over your head, symbolizing the truth you are presenting at that time.

31
Armed Forces' Mottos Preach the Gospel
Matthew 16:24

The five branches of the United States Armed Services are the Navy, the Army, the Air Force, the Coast Guard, and the Marine Corps. The mottos of each of these armed services tell how to live for God.

The Navy's motto is: "Not Self, but Country." The motto for the Christian is: "Not Self, but God"; and it is found in Matthew 16:24, where Jesus said, "If any man will come after me, let him deny himself, and take up his cross, and follow me."

God ought to always be first in life—above people, possessions, and pleasure.

The Army's motto is: "This We'll Defend." This motto for the Christian is found in Jude 1:3, which states, "Fight hard for the faith that was given the holy people of God once and for all time" (NCV).

What are Christians to defend? Defend the work of Jesus Christ on the cross for man's salvation. Defend Jesus' death, burial and resurrection. Defend the truth that salvation is in Jesus alone.

A second motto used by the Army is: "Be All You Can Be." This should also be the Christian's motto. You can only be the best you can be by walking with Jesus through life.

The Air Force's motto is: "Aim High." This is a wonderful motto for the Christian, and it is found in Colossians 3:2: "Set your affection on things above, not on things on the earth."

Aim High to soar above the wrong crowd, to live on a higher plane with God, to know God's plan for your life, to live a clean life, to accomplish great things for God, and to be different from the world.

The Coast Guard's motto is: "Always Ready." This motto brings to mind Paul Revere's Minute Men who were ready to jump into action at any moment to fight the British.

This motto for the Christian is found in I Peter 3:15, which states, "Be ready always." Christians must always be ready to do what God says, go where God sends, and say what God instructs.

Be ready to answer His call to be a missionary, pastor, or evangelist.

Ready to suffer grief or pain,
Ready to stand the test,
Ready to stay at home and send
Others if He sees best.

Ready to go, ready to stay,
Ready my place to fill,
Ready for service, lowly or great,
Ready to do His will.

Ready to speak, ready to warn,
Ready o'er souls to yearn,
Ready in life, ready in death,
Ready for His return. [13]

Always be READY to do what God says, regardless of its cost!

The Marine Corps' motto is: "Always Faithful." This motto for the Christian is found in Revelation 2:10, "be thou faithful unto death." That is, live for Jesus consistently through life.

Jesus is not only good to live for as children, but as teens and adults! Never turn your back on Him. Stay true to Jesus all your life.

As a Christian, you are a soldier in the Lord's army—therefore:

With the Navy sailor, put God and others above self.

With the Army soldier, defend the faith and be all you can be for God.

With the Air Force airman, aim high; don't settle for less than your best for God.

With the Coast Guard sailor, always be ready to go where God sends and do what God says.

With the Marine Corps marine, always be faithful to God and never quit living for Jesus.

Are you a soldier in the Lord's army? Remember the armed service mottos and apply them to living for Jesus.

Prop: Armed Forces flags. As each of the armed forces' talking point is presented, hold its flag.

32
What Salvation Is Like
2 Peter 3:9

Jesus used many objects to explain how a person is saved, how one becomes a Christian.[14]

He said that being saved is like **Opening a Door** to allow Someone to enter. In Revelation 3:20, Jesus states, "Behold, I stand at the door, and knock: if any man hear my voice, and open the door, I will come in to him." Jesus stands knocking at your heart's door so He can enter. He wants to forgive your sin and become your Lord and Savior.

What must a person do to allow Jesus to enter his life? Simply open the door. How does one do that? By faith and repentance (Acts 20:21). Simply pray, "Lord Jesus, come into my life and take away my sin. I want to live for You alone all my life. Amen." Salvation is opening the door of your heart to Jesus and letting Him enter.

Salvation is like **Receiving a Gift.** "The gift of God is eternal life through Jesus Christ our Lord" (Romans 6:23).

I have a gift to give a friend. What must that friend do for the gift to become his? Simply take it. The friend doesn't have to work for it or pay for it. He doesn't have to earn it or even shout for it. All that is necessary for the gift to become his is to receive it. All a person has to do in order for me to keep the gift is nothing.

The same is true regarding the gift of salvation (cleansing of sin and rightness with God). It simply needs to be received. Though salvation is absolutely free, it can never be possessed until it is accepted. Salvation is receiving God's gift of eternal life—a gift that you neither earned nor deserved.

Salvation is like **Accepting an Invitation.** Jesus told a parable (story) of a man who "made a great supper and invited many" to attend (Luke 14:16 WBT). To attend the supper, all the people had to do was accept the invitation. It was not necessary for them to dress up or down; they just had to come.

God has issued a clear invitation to the world to be saved (Romans 10:13). All a person has to do is act upon the invitation to become a child of God. A person does not have to become better or do more good things; he just has to accept the invitation to be saved. Salvation is accepting God's invitation to become His child (1 John 3:1).

Salvation is like **Taking a Bath.** I hope all of you are taking a bath daily, whether or not you need one. Jesus tells us that salvation is like taking a bath. "Not by works of righteousness which we have done, but according to his mercy he saved us, by the washing of regeneration, and renewing of the Holy Ghost" (Titus 3:5).

Dial soap washes the body clean on the outside. Jesus' blood washes the heart clean on the inside. Salvation is allowing Jesus entrance into the heart to wash away the dirt of sin that separates us from God. Salvation is allowing Jesus to wash away sin (disobedient acts like breaking the Ten Commandments) and become our Lord and Savior.

Salvation is like **Drinking Water.** Revelation 22:17 states, "And the Spirit and the bride say, Come. And let him that heareth say, Come. And let him that is athirst come. And whosoever will, let him take the water of life freely." Jesus says that becoming a Christian is like drinking water.

It is when a person is thirsty that water is wanted. In the same way, it is when a person is spiritually thirsty, that is, he realizes he is lost (unsaved) and separated from God, that he is thirsty for the Lord and can be saved. Salvation is letting Jesus fill the spiritual thirst in the heart.

Salvation is like **Entering a Door.** Imagine a huge door that leads to a supply room. The only way to get the supplies in that room is by going through that door. That is the way to have everything inside that room.

Jesus said that salvation is like entering a door. "I am the door: by me if any man enter in, he shall be saved" (John 10:9). Inside Salvation's Door is forgiveness of sin (wrongdoing), happiness, purpose, and Heaven. There is no way to have what is inside the Door unless you enter it. Salvation is entering the Door that leads to God.

Salvation is like **Choosing a Path** to follow. Make sure the path you follow leads to where you want to go. If you get on the wrong path, you may become lost. It's important to know where a path goes before following it.

Jesus says that salvation is like choosing the right path to go. "Enter ye in at the strait gate: for wide is the gate, and broad is the way, that leadeth to destruction, and many there be which go in thereat: Because strait is the gate, and narrow is the way, which leadeth unto life, and few there be that find it" (Matthew 7:13–14). The narrow path is one of forgiveness of sin, fellowship with Jesus, joy, and Heaven. A person gets on the narrow path the moment he receives Christ as Lord and Savior. Salvation is getting on the right path through reception of Jesus as Lord and Savior.

In review, Jesus says salvation is like opening a door to let Someone enter, receiving a gift, accepting an invitation, taking a bath, drinking water, entering a door, and choosing a path to follow. Right now, open the *door* of your heart for Jesus to enter; take God's *gift* of eternal life; accept God's *invitation* to be His child; let Jesus give you a *spiritual bath*; *drink* from God's fountain of eternal life; enter through the *"Door Jesus"* to be saved; *choose* the narrow path to follow.

Prop: A door, a wrapped gift, an invitation, a bar of soap, a bottle of water, and two paths drawn on large posterboard.

33
A Prayer Sandwich
Matthew 6:9–13

Have you ever made a sandwich? Do you like peanut butter and jelly sandwiches? What must be put on bread to make a peanut butter and jelly sandwich? Peanut butter and jelly, of course.

Let's make a "Prayer Sandwich." It will not be a sandwich to eat, but one to keep in the heart. Jesus gives the recipe for such a sandwich in Matthew 6:9-13. In this passage of Scripture, Jesus instructs us to include in our prayers (prayer sandwich) a petition or request for several things.

The first thing to go on the prayer sandwich is to pray for **God's Person** to be reverenced. "Hallowed be Thy name." Pray that God's name (it speaks of who God is) will be treated with respect and reverence.

Pray that **God's Program** will be expanded. "Thy kingdom come." Pray that's God's rule will encompass the whole world and that there will be less and less sin and more and more people who love Jesus. Wouldn't it really be great if everybody loved Jesus and lived for Him? Pray that this will happen. Pray for family members, friends, and others to be saved.

Pray that **God's Plan** will be accomplished. "Thy will be done." Pray that what God wants to do in, with, and through your life will be done. Pray that God's divine desire will be fulfilled with all people and nations.

Pray for **God's Provision** to be given. "Give us this day our daily bread." Pray that all needs will be supplied. In sickness, ask Him to give health; in times of loneliness, ask

Him to give a friend; in times of hunger, ask Him to give food; and in times of sorrow, ask Him to give comfort. You can trust Him to meet every need. There is no need to worry about tomorrow, for God is in control of it, as He is of today.

Pray for **God's Pardon** to be known. "Forgive us our debts, as we forgive our debtors." In the same way that God forgives us, though it is underserved, we are to forgive others even when they don't deserve it. Forgive others and daily ask God to forgive you.

Pray that **God's Prevention** will be experienced. "And lead us not into temptation." Pray that God will not just keep you from sin, but also from the temptation that causes it.

Pray for **God's Protection** to be demonstrated. "But deliver us from the evil one" (NIV). We are to pray that God will not allow Satan to bring us harm. "Greater is he that is in you, than he that is in the world" (1 John 4:4). God provides the power and strength necessary to defeat Satan.

Pray that **God's Praise** will be exhibited. "For thine is the kingdom, and the power, and the glory, for ever. Amen." The model prayer ends with a doxology of praise. Praise is giving God the honor that is due Him. Close prayers with telling God how much you love, honor, and appreciate Him.

Prop: Take two slices of bread (made of Styrofoam) and eight large poster cards (marked with key elements of your talk) into the pulpit. Insert between the slices of "bread" each card as its point is discussed.

34
Policemen
Proverbs 4:23

A policeman is a guard who makes sure people and their possessions are kept safe. In a way, all boys and girls are policemen, in that they are to constantly police their lives to make sure nothing enters that will bring harm. What are some things that God wants you to police?

Police **the tongue** in what you say. Never speak unkind words about another person. Use the tongue to lift people up, not to tear them down; to speak the truth regardless of the cost; to speak much of Jesus and what He did on the cross to make salvation possible for all people. As God's policeman, it is your job to control how you use the tongue.

Police **the mind** in what you think. Don't allow the garbage of the world to enter your mind. As God's policeman, it's your job to chase every bad thought away.

Police **the feet** in where they go. Don't allow your feet to take you down a wrong path. At the instant your feet begin to lead you astray, blow the whistle of warning and turn around. David said, "I have refrained my feet from every evil way, that I might keep thy word" (Psalm 119:101). Refuse to go into places where beer is being consumed, bad movies are being shown, or drugs are being used.

Police **the eyes** in what they see. Don't watch bad movies that stir up wrong kinds of feelings and desires. Police the books and magazines you read to make sure they are healthy and profitable.

Police **the hands** in what you do. Keep your hands free from doing anything wrong. Blow the whistle the moment your hands start to pick up a can of beer, a cigarette, a drug, or a bad magazine. Use your hands to help others, not to hurt them.

Police **the ears** in what they hear. If a friend wants to share a dirty joke, walk away. When Satan whispers in the ear that you are a nobody, that you are worthless, unloved, with no potential, turn away. Police your ears and refuse to let anything enter that brings harm.

A policeman must always be vigilant and alert, ready to blow his whistle, radio for backup, or sound the siren at the sight of wrongdoing. You must also be alert as God's policeman.

Prop: Dress in the uniform of a policeman, complete with whistle and badge.

35
Lessons from the Automobile
Proverbs 3:5–6

Your life is like a car in that it needs five things to get you where God wants you to go.

You need **Brakes.** Brakes stop a car. Without brakes there would be many cars crashing into each other.

Your conscience serves as the brakes on the car of your life, and when it tells you not to do something, you had better stop at once, or else injury could occur. The conscience is that thing in the mind that whistles, buzzes, shouts to you not to do something that is wrong.

You need a **Steering Wheel.** The steering wheel "steers" a car in the direction it is to go. Without a steering wheel a car would be out of control, going wherever it wanted and eventually wrecking.

The Bible is man's "steering wheel." It will take the car of our life in the right direction. The psalmist cried, "Order my steps in thy word" (Psalm 119:133). Another way of putting what he said goes like this, "O God, may the Bible always be the steering wheel of my life so I may go where you want me to be."

David also said, "Thy Word is a lamp unto my feet, and a light unto my path" (Psalm 119:105). Say with David, "Thy Word is the steering wheel of my life that erases the dark and makes clear the way I am to go."

The Bible can only be our Steering Wheel to the degree that we master what it teaches. Study the Bible inside and out until it dwells in you richly, until what is written in its pages is inscribed upon the wall of your heart.

You need a **Windshield.** The windshield of the car is bigger than the rearview mirrors, indicating that the driver should spend more time looking at what is ahead than what is behind.

This is also true for your life car. Focus on what is ahead instead of looking at what is in the past. Paul the Apostle said, "No, dear brothers and sisters, I have not achieved it, but I focus on this one thing: Forgetting the past and looking forward to what lies ahead" (Philippians 3:13).

You need **Windshield Wipers.** Windshield wipers help keep the windshield clean so one can see what is ahead. Do you think anybody would wipe mud all over the windshield of his car prior to driving? He would be foolish and would probably get hurt. The driver of a car has to use windshield wipers to keep the windshield clean so he can see clearly.

The windshield of our life is the heart, and its windshield wipers are prayer. If dirt (sin) gets into our hearts, we cannot see clearly the way to go. The way to get the dirt (sin) off the windshield of your heart is by using the windshield wipers of prayer.

Jesus said, "If we confess our sins, he is faithful and just to forgive us our sins, and to cleanse us from all unrighteousness" (1 John 1:9). Express sorrow to Jesus for doing what you did that was wrong, and ask Him to cleanse it out of your life.

You need an **Engine.** A car has to have power to move, and the power source is called the engine.

The power source (engine) of the Christian's life is the Holy Spirit. The Holy Spirit lives in the Christian, enabling him to go in the direction the Bible instructs. The Holy Spirit also helps the Christian to obey God, avoid doing wrong, and tell others of Jesus.

You need **Lights.** Lights are standard equipment on cars. Lights make it possible for a car to travel when it is pitch black at night. It is important for a driver to use the car's lights at night to avoid an accident.

Christians need lights to light up the road of life to avoid wrecking and possible injury. Who and what are these lights? The lights are Christian friends, parents, Bible teachers, ministers, children's workers, Sunday school, church services, and sermons. God wants to use people and places like these to help you live a wonderful life pleasing unto Him.

Car equipment like brakes, steering wheel, windshield, windshield wipers, engine, and lights can only do the driver good if they are used. Likewise, for our spiritual car equipment to bear any benefit, they must be utilized.

Prop: A big model car and a cutout of a car labeled "car of life." Hold the car in your hand throughout the talk.

36
Keep Off This Seat
Psalm 1:1

Sometimes on a broken bench or chair, a sign will be posted that states: "Keep Off This Seat." Failure to obey this warning could result in one's getting injured. Did you know that God has posted some "Keep Off This Seat" signs in the Bible?

One of these signs reads: "Keep Off This Seat" regarding **being scornful.** "Blessed is the man that walketh not in the counsel of the ungodly, nor standeth in the way of sinners, nor sitteth in the seat of the scornful" (Psalm 1:1).

To be scornful means to make fun of prayer, the church, God, the Bible, people who love Jesus, pastors, and anything else that has to do with religion. God says, "Do not sit in this seat." Choose not be around people who make fun of spiritual things.

A second sign reads: "Keep Off This Seat" regarding **bad friends.** "Enter not into the path of the wicked, and go not in the way of evil men" (Proverbs 4:14).

Amnon "had a friend, whose name was Jonadab" who helped him do something that was very bad (2 Samuel 13:3) when he could have urged him to do what was right. He was a bad friend. Amnon should have chosen his friends more wisely having 'kept off this seat' of bad friends.

Choose your friends cautiously and carefully, unlike Amnon. Make sure a person you want to be your friend loves Jesus, does not do bad things like drinking beer, using drugs, looking at bad magazines, or using bad words. The right kind of friend would never try to get you to do something that was wrong.

Another sign reads: "Keep Off This Seat" regarding **your parents.** "Foolish children bring grief to their fathers and bitter regrets to their mothers" (Proverbs 17:25 GNT). That is, "Do not sit in the seat of rebellion toward your parents, for it brings great pain to them."

The apostle Paul urges, "Children, obey your parents in the Lord: for this is right" (Ephesians 6:1). The fifth Commandment instructs children to "Honour thy father and thy mother: that thy days may be long upon the land which the LORD thy God giveth thee" (Exodus 20:12).

How can you stay out of the seat of rebellion to your parents? By going where your parents send you, doing what they say immediately, without argument, cheerfully, and showing them utmost respect. Always honor your parents with your lips and with you life. Others may sit in the seat of rebellion toward their parents, but determine that you will not.

A fourth sign reads: "Keep Off This Seat" regarding the **church.** "Not forsaking the assembling of ourselves together, as the manner of some is; but exhorting one another: and so much the more, as ye see the day approaching" (Hebrews 10:25). That is, "Do not sit in the seat of neglect of the church just because others do."

The gigantic Redwood trees have shallow roots. Roots are like anchors to a tree, keeping it from falling to the ground. How then can these huge trees stand without falling? The trees intertwine their roots with each other, drawing strength from each other to stand.

You have shallow roots spiritually, and you will fall down spiritually, unless you go to church and allow the roots of other Christians to wrap around yours, making you strong. Every Christian needs other believers to help him or her grow up in the faith.

The next sign reads: "Keep Off This Seat" regarding **sexual misconduct.** "God wants you to live a pure life. Keep yourselves from sexual promiscuity" (I Thessalonians 4:3 The Message).

Sex is something that is to take place in a marriage relationship between a husband and a wife, so refuse to sit in this seat. Keep yourself pure in mind and body, free from sexual sin.

Another sign reads: "Keep Off This Seat" regarding **dishonesty.** Always do right, though the stars fall from the sky. Honesty is not only the best policy, it is the only policy. Don't cheat on tests, tell lies, steal, or fail to do what you say.

A final sign which you need to heed reads: "Keep Off This Seat" regarding **pornography.** Pornography is a big word that is used to describe books, magazines, pictures, or movies that are bad.

Don't sit in this seat. Refuse to look at pornography, and keep your mind clean from the trash which the world and the Devil want to dump in it.

Regarding all these things, God has erected a sign clearly saying: "Keep Off This Seat." If you ignore the sign and engage in these things, you will not only be disobeying God, but you will hurt yourself as well.

Prop: Seven chairs, seven "Keep Off This Seat" signs, and a banner made for each of the talking points. Place a "Keep Off This Seat" sign on each of the seven chairs on the platform. As you speak, place the banner of each point on a chair.

37
Wrong Uses of the Tongue—Part One
Proverbs 21:23

In the classic movie *A Christmas Story,* during recess on a cold winter day, two boys surrounded by classmates argue whether a person's tongue will stick to the school's flagpole. One of the boys "triple-dog dares" the other to stick his tongue to the pole, and it gets stuck. As his classmates returned to class, there he remained with his tongue frozen to the flagpole in great pain. Of all the right uses of the tongue, this certainly was not one of them!

This humorous scene points out how the tongue brings trouble and pain when misused. Solomon said, "Whoso keepeth his mouth and his tongue keepeth his soul from troubles" (Proverbs 21:23). Or, as The Message translation puts it, "Watch your words and hold your tongue; you'll save yourself a lot of grief."

Whereas most students would not intentionally hurt another physically, they often do so mentally with the use of a vicious tongue. The Bible speaks of the kind of tongues that that must be avoided because they will hurt God, others, and us personally.

Avoid a Harsh Tongue. "A soft answer turns away wrath, but a harsh word stirs up anger" (Proverbs 15:1 ESV). I remember as a child saying to someone who said something unkind to me, "Sticks and stones may break my bones, but words will never hurt me." I don't know why I ever said that, because their harsh words did hurt me. Harsh words are but an invisible sharp razor that cuts and pains deeply the person on the receiving end (Psalm 52: 2).

Avoid a Lying Tongue. "The getting of treasures by a lying tongue is a vanity tossed to and fro of them that seek death" (Proverbs 21:6). In order to gain possessions, popularity, and friends, or to avoid punishment for acts committed, lies often are told.

A lying tongue is condemned by God. Always speak the truth despite the consequence.

Avoid a Belittling Tongue. "Do not use harmful words, but only helpful words, the kind that build up and provide what is needed, so that what you say will do good to those who hear you" (Ephesians 4:29 GNT). Never speak to someone in a way that makes them think they are a nobody. Words ought to lift another up, not pull them down. Who might you, without realizing it, be belittling with words?

Avoid a Betraying Tongue. "A gossip goes around revealing secrets, but those who are trustworthy can keep a confidence" (Proverbs 11:13 NLT). Simply put, Solomon is saying, "Don't divulge what others have told in confidentiality, and never share such to hurt them openly." Determine to be a person who is trustworthy with secrets.

Avoid a Retaliating Tongue. "Don't repay evil for evil. Don't retaliate when people say unkind things about you. Instead, pay them back with a blessing. That is what God wants you to do, and he will bless you for it" (I Peter 3:9, NLT). Or, as The Message puts it, "That goes for all of you, no exceptions. No retaliation. No sharp-tongued sarcasm. Instead, bless—that's your job, to bless. You'll be a blessing and also get a blessing."

When you are offended or injured by another's actions, restrain from striking back to get even. This is most difficult, for the flesh craves to even the score, but God says, "Don't do it; leave the matter to Me to handle."

God commands that we bless people who injure us. How can we do that? We bless others by praying for their salvation or spiritual progress, expressing thankfulness for them, doing something to help them, and speaking well of them. God states that if we do that, not only will that person's life be enriched, but ours will be richer as well.

> "You can talk about me,
> As much as you please;
> I'll talk about you;
> Down on my knees."

Envision that in my hand is a pillow and that the thousands of feathers in it are words. What is the likelihood of replacing every single feather, if they once are blown in every direction by powerful fans? It is very unlikely.

Words are like such feathers; once spoken, they never can be taken back. Never use the tongue in these negative manners, and you will never be sorry for what you say.

Prop: A large tongue cut out of posterboard or Styrofoam, and attachments (names of each type of tongue). Attach each type of tongue to the large tongue as it is discussed.

The use of a dandelion flower (in the white gray seed stage) may illustrate the impossibility of retracting words (once the flower's seeds are blown away, they never can be brought back). Cited at the conclusion of Part Two is a suggestion regarding the pillow illustration.

38
Wrong Uses of the Tongue—Part Two
Proverbs 21:23

There are five more bad tongues to avoid.

Avoid a Hasty Tongue. "Seest thou a man that is hasty in his words? there is more hope of a fool than of him" (Proverbs 29:20). "He that refraineth his lips is wise" (Proverbs 10:19).

Be slow to speak, and learn when to be silent. When are the times that a person needs to refrain from speaking?

Hold the tongue when you are spoken to by someone who is angry.

Don't answer hurriedly when you are asked to do something that requires thoughtfulness and prayer, for you could agree to do something that you would later regret doing, or you could decline to do something that you would later wish you had done.

When you are being corrected by a parent or teacher, hold the tongue and refrain from justifying the wrong that you have committed.

Hold the tongue when a parent gets on your case about something you count as petty. Remember, hasty speaking may lead to speaking words that will later be regretted.

Avoid a Grumbling Tongue. "And when the people complained, it displeased the LORD: and the LORD heard it" (Numbers 11:1). To God's displeasure, the Israelites complained and grumbled in the wilderness about the manner in which He provided for them.

There are few things worse than hearing Christians grumble and complain, in light of all God has done and is doing for them. The chorus to "The Grumbler's Song" describes them:

Oh, they grumble on Monday, Tuesday, Wednesday, grumble on Thursday too.

They grumble on Friday, Saturday, Sunday, grumble the whole week through.

In light of God's gracious provision, Solomon asks a most pressing question: "Then why should we, mere humans, complain..." (Lamentations 3:39 NLT).

Instead of complaining and whining, use the tongue to worship, adore, and praise God for all He has done and is doing for you. Nobody likes to be around a grumbler—not even God!

Avoid a Hollow Tongue. "A flattering mouth worketh ruin" (Proverbs 26:28). Don't speak words of insincerity. Don't speak empty words. Be careful not to use the hollow tongue to praise people in order to gain approval or support. There is nothing wrong with sharing genuine, heartfelt compliments; just avoid stretching the truth, wherein it becomes a lie.

Avoid a Divisive Tongue. "he that soweth discord among brethren" (Proverbs 6:19). One of the things on this list of seven things that God hates is a person who uses the tongue to create dissension and discord.

You sow discord by saying things that break bonds of friendship, promote cliques ("we four and no more"), polarize (create a rift) one person from another, and decay the trust that someone has in another.

Avoid a Discouraging Tongue. "And Judah said, The strength of the bearers of burdens is decayed, and there is much rubbish; so that we are not able to build the wall" (Nehemiah 4:10). Nehemiah was trying to rebuild the walls about Jerusalem and reestablish God's worship, which was opposed greatly. As if things were not difficult enough for Nehemiah, his right hand man, Judah, spoke discouragingly, saying their effort was useless and they should quit.

These words from Judah's mouth were like a sword to Nehemiah's heart. It has to be disheartening when a trusted friend who should be inflating you to do what God has purposed deflates you instead.

Don't use the tongue to discourage others from doing what God has placed in their hearts to do. If someone says God has called him or her to be a missionary, don't respond by saying, "You don't have what it takes to be a missionary"; rather, say, "I believe you will make a good one." If someone says he or she is going to start a Bible Club at school, don't say, "Sure. That will be the day"; instead, say, "I was hoping someone would start a club, and I am glad you are that person." If another says, "I am inviting Jesus into my heart to be my Lord and Savior," don't say, "I can't believe you are doing that"; respond with, "I am so happy for you. Becoming a Christian is awesome." Or if one states the intention to quit a certain sinful act (pornography, drugs, alcohol, gambling, sexual impurity, etc.), never respond, "You can't stop that. You can't change. You have tried before and failed. You can't do it now either." Tell such a person, "I know you tried to stop before, but I believe this time you will succeed with God's help."

Don't be a Judah. Rather, use the tongue to encourage people to do all God has placed in their hearts to accomplish. I wonder how many great things for God have not been done because someone discouraged another from attempting to do them.

Prop: A huge tongue (Styrofoam) and attachable placards bearing the names of each tongue discussed, and a feathered pillow-case.

Option 2: Draw a tongue on the feather pillow. Insert in the pillow the various tongues in the talk. Take each type of tongue out of the pillow as you discuss it. This option makes the feather-pillow illustration even more effective. I opened this second sermon by asking the children to name the bad tongues discussed in Part 1.

39
Muzzling the Tongue
Psalm 39:1

When you see a doctor, the first thing you are asked to do is to stick out the tongue. The tongue reveals much about a person's health.

It also reveals much about spiritual health, for what we say lives first in the heart. You see, all the filth and disrespect and foul talk one does lives first in the heart and then comes out through the lips. The heart is a well, and the lips are its faucet. Whatever is in the well flows out the faucet. So a key to controlling the tongue is keeping the "heart-well" pure and clean.

To my knowledge, though doctors can replace arms and legs, they cannot replace the tongue. The tongue you were born with will never change, so make up your mind to use it rightly. How can the tongue be muzzled?

David states, "I will guard my ways, that I may not sin with my tongue; I will guard my mouth with a muzzle" (Psalm 39:1 ESV). How can you muzzle your mouth to say only things pleasing to God?

It takes **Decision.** Decide to obey God and speak only things that help others rather than hurting them. Decide to talk right to Mom and Dad and friends; Don't speak in an ugly way.

It takes **Devotion.** Love Jesus with all your heart and delight to please Him in all you say and do. Fill your mind with Bible truth, and always stay close to Jesus.

It takes **Dependence.** James tells us that no man can tame the tongue (James 3:8). And he is right—but Jesus can.

So rely upon His super-duper-natural strength to help you speak rightly.

It takes **Discipline.** Don't "give place to the devil" (Ephesians 4:27); that is, don't condone any bad talk at any time about any person. Always say a loud no to bad talk.

It takes **Direction.** You need to know *how* to speak rightly and not wrongly. The word T.H.I.N.K[15] is such a guide. Each of its letters helps us know how to use the tongue in a way pleasing to God.

T—Is it true? If not, don't speak it.
H—Is it helpful or hurtful?
I—Is it inspiring, uplifting, encouraging?
N—Is it really necessary to say? Much of what is said to others about others is best left unsaid.
K—Is it kind or ugly?
Is it true, helpful, inspirational, necessary, and kind? If not, don't say it.

We all need to muzzle, bridle, control our tongue and use it more to tell others about Jesus and His awesome love. THINK before you speak.

Prop: Cut out the letters of the word THINK and hold each one as you explain its meaning in relation to the talk. Additionally, a dog muzzle may be used to illustrate the meaning of muzzle.

40

How to Make the Best of Life
John 10:10

Jesus not only wants you to go to Heaven; He wants you to make the best of your life on the way there. Hear what He states: "I am come that they might have life, and that they might have it more abundantly [fuller, richer, fulfilling, meaningful, joyous]" (John 10:10).

There are six things necessary to make the best of life here and now.

The first thing is to **Live a Good Life.** A worthwhile life begins with knowing Jesus, for it is impossible to live life at its best without Him in control. *Good* cannot be spelled without including *God,* and you cannot live a good life without God. Always do right, though the stars fall from the sky.

The second thing to do is **Live a Growing Life.** As you grow physically, also grow spiritually. Keep doing what it takes to grow up in Jesus. Never stop praying, studying the Bible, going to church, reading Christian literature, and resisting temptation.

Third, **Live a Guarded Life.** Peter warns, "Be sober, be vigilant; because your adversary the devil, as a roaring lion, walketh about, seeking whom he may devour: Whom resist stedfast in the faith, knowing that the same afflictions are accomplished in your brethren that are in the world" (1 Peter 5:8–9). Satan will try to stop you from living for Jesus. Be cautious not to allow any person or thing into your life that will harm your walk with Jesus.

Paul the apostle shares the key to living a guarded life in Ephesians.

"So take everything the Master has set out for you, well-made weapons of the best materials. And put them to use so you will be able to stand up to everything the Devil throws your way.

"This is no afternoon athletic contest that we'll walk away from and forget about in a couple of hours. This is for keeps, a life-or-death fight to the finish against the Devil and all his angels.

"Be prepared. You're up against far more than you can handle on your own. Take all the help you can get, every weapon God has issued, so that when it's all over but the shouting you'll still be on your feet.

"Truth, righteousness, peace, faith, and salvation are more than words. Learn how to apply them. You'll need them throughout your life. God's Word is an indispensable weapon.

"In the same way, prayer is essential in this ongoing warfare. Pray hard and long. Pray for your brothers and sisters. Keep your eyes open. Keep each other's spirits up so that no one falls behind or drops out."—Ephesians 6:11–18 The Message.

Paul says the key to a guarded life is the wearing of the gospel armor every day. Discipline yourself to put it on each morning the rest of your life.

Be sure to **Live a Guided Life.** Solomon declared, "In all thy ways acknowledge him [God], and he shall direct thy paths" (Proverbs 3:6).

There is a song that states, "Each step I take, I take in you. You are my way, Jesus." God wants to direct each step of your life regarding marriage, life's work (missionary, pastor, evangelist, youth, music, etc.), and every other detail of life.

As a youth, I recall singing,

I place my life in the hands of God,
In those hands now outstretched for me.
Wherever it may be, over land, over sea,
May Thy will sublime, O thou God divine, be mine.

Place your life in God's hands, letting Him guide you through life's journey so that you will not go astray.

Next, **Live a Giving Life.** Jesus is the world's greatest giver. He loved the world so much that He gave His very best to provide forgiveness of sin so man might know God, live life to its fullest, and one day have Heaven.

Let's be givers. Jesus said, "Freely ye have received, freely give" (Matthew 10:8). Freely give of your love, time, possessions, talents, and money to help others.

Don't live a self-centered life, a life consumed with making yourself happy. Make it your goal to make others happy, and you will find happiness beyond measure.

Finally, **Live a Going Life.** To live a worthwhile life, it's important to go and tell others of God's awesome love as demonstrated at Calvary. You are not too young to start going and telling.

There is nothing any more wonderful then helping another find salvation in Jesus Christ (Acts 1:8). These six things will enable you to live a life of purpose and happiness.

Prop: A large circle cut out of posterboard entitled LIFE. As each talking point is discussed, attach that point to the circle—Good, Growing, Guarded, Guided, Giving, Going—each directed toward the word LIFE in the circle.

41
Boats in Your Heart
2 Peter 2:18

At a South Carolina lake, there are boats tied to the dock waiting to take people to the cross at the other side of the lake. But guess what? The boats will never take a person to the cross if he doesn't first get into the boat and paddle to it. The gain is worth the effort.

There are six spiritual boats that God wants Christians to board that will provide transportation into His presence, enabling greater love for Him and knowledge of Him.

There is the **boat of prayer.** Board the boat of prayer daily, for it is the key to walking with the Lord. Prayer is simply talking to God. It might be helpful to use the prayers in the Psalms to get started praying. God says, "Ye have not, because ye ask not" (James 4:2). Ask big and great things from God.

There is the **boat of Scripture.** The boat of Scripture is God's Word to you, true and sound to prosper you. It's a lamp unto your path and food unto your soul, so feed on it continually that you may fully grow. Each morning, start the day riding in this boat of quiet time with the Lord.

There is the **boat of soul winning.** Tell others the message of the cross so they too can know Jesus. Do you know who the Geico insurance company spokesman is? A lizard. One commercial shows the lizard challenging a lot of lizards to spread the word about Geico insurance, because, he states, "It's that important." God wants us to spread the Word about Calvary, because it's that important.

There is the **boat of solitude.** That's a big word. It means to be in a quiet place with Jesus so you can think and meditate. It is a place where the television, radio, or CD is not playing and you are not gathered with friends. It is just Jesus and you having fellowship. The best part of the day is not waking up to Folgers in your cup (coffee), but meeting with Jesus.

There is the **boat of journaling.** Some keep diaries about friends, family, and fun times. A journal is a type of diary about God and you. Start now to write down what is learned from studying the Bible and hearing sermons. It's easy to forget some awesome stuff you learned about God, so write it down.

There is the **boat of stewardship.** Give of your time, talent and treasure (money) to God. Never be greedy with God. A person can never outgive the Lord.

These six boats will lead to a place of knowing God better. Board them regularly.

Prop: Six toy boats, each one inscribed with one of the names of the different kinds of boats. Hold each boat when it is being discussed.

42

Good and Bad Seed—Part One
Galatians 6:7

If you have a pack of flower seeds, what is necessary to do in order to get a beautiful flower? Plant them in dirt and water them.

Can flower seeds produce an apple or a coconut tree? No, because a seed can produce only what it came from. If you want flowers, plant flower seeds; if you want an apple tree, plant apple seeds; and if you want coconuts, plant coconut seeds. What you plant is what you will get every time.

The same is true with regard to the heart. Plant good seeds in order to reap what is good; plant bad seeds in order to reap what is hurtful. Refuse to plant bad seeds in the heart or allow anyone else to do so. We plant seeds in the heart by doing that which is good or bad, and we water the seeds by continuing to do good or bad.

What are some bad seed that must be avoided, not planted in the heart?

Don't plant the bad seed of **Pornography.** Pornography refers to books, magazines, movies, videos, and Internet web sites about people doing things that are bad sexually. Don't allow this seed to be planted in your heart, for if it is, it will grow up to steal your happiness and peace.

Don't plant the bad seed of **Tobacco.** Tobacco in any form will destroy a person's health. Once the tobacco seed is planted, it is very difficult to pluck up (remove).

Don't plant the bad seed of **Disobedience to Parents.** Disobedience to your parents will lead to harmful consequences, while obedience to them will enable you to live a happier and longer life. You plant the good seed of obedience in your heart by coming when your parents call you, going where they send you, doing what they tell you, and doing it promptly and cheerfully.

Don't plant the bad seed of **Dishonesty.** Each time you tell a lie, take something that doesn't belong to you, cheat on a test, or cheat in a game, you are planting the bad seed of dishonesty in your life.

Grover Cleveland, when a young boy, insisted on returning eggs that a neighbor's hen had laid on his family's side of the fence. This seed of honesty he planted in his heart at such an early age led him to be honest in all matters as he grew older. Eventually, it was his honesty that marked him to become a president of the United States.

Sow the seed of honesty in your heart by always doing the honest thing at school, while you are playing, or when you are at home, regardless of the cost. As with President Cleveland, have a reputation of honesty.

> The world is anxious to employ
> Not just one, but every boy
> Whose heart and brain will e'er be true
> To work his hands shall find to do.
> Honest, faithful, earnest, kind,
> To good awake, to evil blind,
> Heart of gold, without alloy—
> Wanted—the world wants such a boy.[16]

Don't plant the bad seed of **Hate.** Refuse to hate anyone. Be forgiving to everyone, seventy times seven times. Don't hold grudges, but love those who injure you.

Jesus on the cross had nails driven into His hands, a sword to pierce His side, and a crown of thorns pressed upon His head; yet He said, "Father, forgive them; for they know not what they do" (Luke 23:34). Love and forgive like Jesus.

SAND AND STONE

Two friends were walking through the desert. During one point in the journey, they had an argument, and one friend slapped the other one in the face. The one who got slapped was hurt, but without saying anything, she wrote in the sand: "Today, my best friend slapped me in the face."

They kept on walking until they found an oasis. They decided to go swimming. The one who had been slapped got stuck in the mire and started drowning. But her friend saved her. After she recovered from the near drowning, she wrote on a stone: "Today, my best friend saved my life."

The friend who had slapped and then saved her best friend asked, "After I hurt you, you wrote in the sand. And now, you write on the stone. Why?"

The friend replied, "When someone hurts us, we should write it down in the sand where the winds of forgiveness can erase it. But when someone does something good for us, we must engrave it in stone where no wind can ever erase it."

Learn to write your hurts in the sand and to carve your blessings in stone.[17]

Don't plant the bad seed of **Bad Language.** Profanity is using God's name in a bad way. Obscenity is using dirty words. Use neither.

The Bible states, "When you talk, you should always be kind and pleasant so you will be able to answer everyone in the way you should" (Colossians 4:6 NCV). God wants you to use only words that are kind, loving, truthful and wholesome. Because they planted the seed of profanity and obscenity in their lives while they were children, some people can hardly talk without using one of those bad words.

Don't plant the bad seed of **Spiritual Indifference.** Indifference is a big word. It means to be without concern for or interest in something. You plant this seed in your life when reading the Bible, going to church, obeying God, and doing right become unimportant to you. Planting this seed in one's life results in a life that is distant from God. The more it is watered, the further the person moves away from God.

Make your walk with God your top priority. Sow (plant) the good seeds of Bible devotion, prayer, church attendance, and obedience to enable you to grow spiritually.

As flower seeds grow flowers, apple seeds grow apples, and coconut seeds grow coconuts, so bad seed grows bad lives, and good seed grows good lives. Determine to plant only good seed in your life and in the life of others.

Prop: A pack of flower seed and a farmer's apron containing seed. Seven small planting containers or pots filled with dirt and having a twig from a tree, each labeled with one of the talking points. As each point is discussed, throw some seed in its container. Similarly use the pots for Part Two.

43
Good and Bad Seed—Part Two
Galatians 6:7

The Bible states that we can sow (plant) good or bad "heart seeds." These seeds will make us either good or bad.

We plant these seeds in our hearts by doing good things or bad things. Be very careful to plant and let others plant in your heart only good seed.

What are some good seed that you ought to plant in your life?

Plant the good seed of **Salvation.** To invite Jesus Christ into your heart as Lord and Savior is the best decision you can make in your life.

Three colors tell the why and how of salvation. The first color is black, and it stands for sin. The Bible states that "all have sinned, and come short of the glory of God" (Romans 3:23).

Sin is doing wrong things, and all have done wrong. Sin separates us from God's best intentions for life presently, and one day it will keep us out of Heaven.

The second color is red. It stands for the blood of Jesus shed at Calvary, demonstrating God's great love.

He loved you enough that He gave His one and only Son to die on a cross to make possible forgiveness and rightness with God.

The white color stands for the cleansing of sin that takes place upon receiving Jesus. Jesus stands knocking upon the door of your heart right now seeking entrance (Revelation 3:20). Open the door, allowing Him to enter.

Plant the good seed of **Scripture.** David, the psalmist, said "Thy word have I hid in mine heart, that I might not sin against thee [God]" (Psalm 119:11).

When you read the Bible and memorize its parts, you are planting its seeds in your life, and they will help you know Jesus better and live for Him victoriously.

Plant the good seed of **Prayer.** Prayer is talking to God. Prayer protects us, provides for us, strengthens us, sustains us, guides us, purifies us, and keeps us close to God.

Keep planting this seed in your life by praying often. The Bible states that "men ought always to pray, and not to faint" (Luke 18:1).

Plant the good seed of **Church Attendance.** Go to church, give to the church, pray for the church, and invite others to come to church. This is good seed to plant in your life and in the lives of others.

The Bible teaches us in Hebrews 10:25 (NCV), "You should not stay away from the church meetings, as some are doing, but you should meet together and encourage each other. Do this even more as you see the day coming."

You are small in stature and weak spiritually, and you need adults to help you grow in knowledge and intimacy with Jesus. Every time you attend church, people plant seeds in your life that enhances Christian growth.

Plant the good seed of **Obedience to God.** It is not only important to read the Bible; you must also do what it says.

A Chinese person was asked what he thought of Christians. He replied, "There is too much talkie-talkie and not enough walkie-walkie."

He is right. It is one thing to *talk* about how much you love Jesus and quite another to *show* how much you love Jesus by doing what He commands.

Trust and obey, for there's no other way
To be happy in Jesus, but to trust and obey.

Be as David, who declared, "I have refrained my feet from every evil way, that I might keep thy word" (Psalm 119:101).

Plant the good seed of **Service.** Jesus wants you to do kind deeds (things) to help and share His love with others.

You say, "But, Brother Frank, I'm just a kid. What can I do for Jesus?" There are many things that someone at your age can do to serve God.

Serve God by participating in a toy wash in the nursery at your church; wash the windshields of cars in the church parking lot during Sunday school; wash dishes at home to help your mother; take flowers to the elderly and the shut-in; be a prayer warrior for a missionary; be a shoebox helper (stuffing shoeboxes) for the Samaritan's Purse's Operation Christmas Child; give slightly used clothing and shoes to the needy; serve God by befriending those who are lonely.

Plant these good seeds in your heart every day. If you have not yet invited Jesus into your life, do that right now.

Prop: See Part One.

44
The Knots of God

Have you ever tied a knot in a pair of shoestrings that couldn't be untied? I certainly have.

God has connected some things together by tying them in such a way that no man can untie them. These are things that go together in the Christian life.

The knot of **repentance and faith** (Acts 20:21). Repentance is a big word that simply means "to change directions." If I am walking in one direction and then turn completely around to walk in another direction, what has happened? I have changed my mind about the direction I was walking; that is, I repented. Biblically, to repent is to change one's mind about sin and God; it is to stop hating and disobeying Him and begin to love and obey Him.

Faith means "to trust." I recall climbing down off the roof of our home as a child, with my dad waiting to catch me. Though he was out of my sight, I trusted him to catch me when I let go of the roof. Biblically faith means a willingness to trust Jesus Christ to forgive sin and save, though He cannot be seen.

God has tied repentance and faith (trust) together as the means of salvation. It takes both a change of mind about sin and trust in Jesus as Lord and Savior.

The knot of **church and baptism** (Acts 2:38). What is baptism? It pictures Jesus' death, burial and resurrection. It is like a silent movie describing what happened to Jesus from Good Friday to Easter Morning. It is Jesus' command that everyone who loves Him be baptized.

Tied to baptism is the church. Pray for the church, support the church, attend the church, give to the church, serve God in the church, and always be faithful to the church. The church is important to spiritual growth and obedience to God.

At conversion to Christ, be baptized and unite with a church. God has tied baptism and the church forever together.

The knot of **lip** (profession) **and lifestyle** (separation) (2 Corinthians 6:17). A Christian backs up what he says with how he lives. Profession and separation are inseparable in the Christian life. A person who loves Jesus lives differently than a person who does not.

The knot of **trusting and telling** (Matthew 10:32–33). Christians want to tell others of their decision to follow Christ. Salvation and sharing, trusting and telling go together. God wants you to tell of His love demonstrated on the cross so others may know Him.

The knot of **salvation and service** (Ephesians 2:8–10). Everyone Jesus saves, He calls to service. Salvation and service are inseparable. Every Christian has a work to do for God.

The knot of **Scripture and supplication** (prayer) (Isaiah 65:24). Scripture is God talking to us; prayer is our talking to God. Both are vital to the Christian life and inseparable.

Prop: For each talking point, take two separate ropes and label each with one side of that talking point; then tie them together. For example: Repentance would be attached to one rope and faith to another; these would be tied together to show their perpetual connection.

144

45
The Hands of Jesus
Isaiah 53:10

"The pleasure of the LORD shall prosper in his hand." Let's look at the hands of Jesus and see what they hold for us.

In His hand is **Salvation:** "And I give unto them eternal life; and they shall never perish, neither shall any man pluck them out of my hand" (John 10:28). Jesus stands with open hands offering forgiveness of sins and eternal life. Neither you nor anyone deserves it, earns it, or in anywise may purchase it. Jesus died for it, and He alone gives it. With open Hands, He waits to give it to you.

In His hand is **Security:** "…neither shall any man pluck them out of my hand" (John 10:28). The word "pluck" means "to rob or seize or snatch away." Jesus is making it clear that once a person enters into His family, absolutely nothing or anyone can force him or her out. The apostle Paul closes out Romans 8 with a hymn of security, filled with questions and answers.

"Can anything ever separate us from Christ's love? Does it mean he no longer loves us if we have trouble or calamity, or are persecuted, or are hungry or cold or in danger or threatened with death?

"(Even the Scriptures say, 'For your sake we are killed every day; we are being slaughtered like sheep.')

"No, despite all these things, overwhelming victory is ours through Christ, who loved us.

"And I am convinced that nothing can ever separate us from his love. Death can't, and life can't. The angels can't, and the demons can't. Our fears for today, our worries about

tomorrow, and even the powers of hell can't keep God's love away.

"Whether we are high above the sky or in the deepest ocean, nothing in all creation will ever be able to separate us from the love of God that is revealed in Christ Jesus our Lord."—Romans 8:35–39 NLT.

Do we need further assurance that Jesus will hedge us in from Satan, preserving us in His salvation? I say absolutely not!

"Behold, I have graven thee upon the palms of my hands" (Isaiah 49:16). Within the wounds in His hands the believer's name is etched. This seals our salvation and forever assures our entrance into Heaven.

In His hand is **Supply:** "But my God shall supply all your need according to his riches in glory by Christ Jesus" (Philippians 4:19). The apostle Paul had experienced poverty at its deepest, hatred at its worst, rejection at its saddest, and death at its cruelest; yet, he says, "My God shall supply all your need according to his riches in glory by Christ Jesus." The Christian never should fret or fear, for in the hands of Jesus is provision for every need. He can do anything but fail you.

In His hand is **Service:** "After these things the Lord appointed other seventy also, and sent them two and two before his face into every city and place, whither he himself would come" (Luke 10:1). Jesus not only saves us from our sin, protects us in our salvation, and supplies our daily needs, but He also dispatches us, issues orders to us regarding His plan for our lives. It is Jesus who assigns what task His children are to do so that the purpose of God may be fulfilled. What might be the call or appointment of God for your life? Might it be to serve as a pastor, missionary, evangelist, music or student

146

minister, chaplain? As Jesus asked Thomas to "behold my hands" (Luke 24:39), He now asks you to do the same so that in beholding them, you may receive gladly, generously, and graciously of all He has provided.

Prop: A hand made out of posterboard with each point written but concealed on one of the fingers until it is discussed.

46
The Fruit of the Spirit
Galatians 5: 22–25

What is the "Heart-Fruit" that the Holy Spirit grows in our hearts that makes us more like Jesus?

Part of it is a "No Matter What" kind of **Love.** God wants you to love others unconditionally as He loves you, regardless of what they say or do and whatever their color or race might be.

Part of it is an "Always Present" kind of **Joy.** God wants you to have joy, no matter what happens around you or to you. Joy is the result of trusting God to take care of you in all situations.

Part of it is an "Unshakeable" kind of **Peace.** God enables you to live in peace on the inside, to experience inner calmness, an inner quietness no matter what happens.

Part of it is a "Job" kind of **Patience.** God wants you to be patient with answers to prayer, problem solving, sickness, and people who irritate, agitate, and upset you.

Part of it is a "Love Shown" kind of **Kindness.** God wants you to be kind to others, treating them gently and lovingly. Do things that make people smile.

Part of it is a "Good Samaritan" kind of **Goodness.** God wants you to do what is right, no matter what the consequences may be. Though the stars fall from the sky, always do what is right and good.

Part of it is a "Promise Is a Promise" kind of **Faithfulness.** God wants you to keep your word and do what you say you will do when you say you will do it.

Part of it is a "Towel and Basin" kind of **Gentleness** (Meekness). Jesus took a towel and a basin of water and washed the disciples' feet. God wants you to treat others with respect, courtesy, and dignity, as Jesus does.

Part of it is a "Joseph" kind of **Self-Control.** God wants us to say no to what is wrong in our words and in our conduct!

Each of these nine parts of the Fruit of the Spirit will grow more and more in you as you obey Jesus, study the Bible, go to church, and pray. But they all begin with knowing Jesus personally as Lord and Savior. Jesus is ever ready to enter your life. Just ask Him and He will.

Prop: A huge heart on which the Fruit of the Spirit may be attached one by one as the talk proceeds.

47
Board Games That Preach

Imagine a big box that contains several board games that teach some spiritual truths.

The first board game in the box is **Sorry**. Always be sorry for doing wrong, hurting others, and displeasing God. The prodigal son is an example of how one ought to express sorrow for doing wrong to others (Luke 15:21).

The next game in the box is **Battleship**. The Christian life is a continuous battle against sin. Satan is relentless in attacking the believer, seeking his destruction (1 Peter 5:8). The Christian can have the victory over Satan by relying upon Jesus (1 John 4:4).

Monopoly is the next board game. Jesus is to monopolize your life, being in total control of what you say and do (Romans 12:1–2). Jesus monopolizes a person's life at the moment it is surrendered totally to Him.

The fourth board game in the box is **Clue**. In this game, a person plays detective, seeking to solve a crime (who did it, where it was committed, and with what weapon). You start the game with some clues of your own, then make guesses to rule out possibilities until finally the crime is solved.

Don't try to live your life the way people play this game—guessing what to do, when to do it, how to do it, and where to do it. You need only one clue to live life to the fullest, and that clue is to look to Jesus (Proverbs 3:5–6; 2 Chronicles 20:12b; Proverbs 25:8a).

The **Trouble** board game is next in the box. Troubles and failures are part and parcel of growing up. The path on which you now walk others have trodden victoriously by looking beyond the moment to the future and holding onto the promise of God that He will neither forsake nor fail His children (Hebrews 13:5).

When a professor asked an African-American pastor, "What is your favorite verse in Scripture?" he replied, "And it came to pass."

The professor replied, "That's not a verse of Scripture. It is only part of a verse."

The pastor countered, "I know. I have lots of troubles and trials at times, but they all come to pass."

Whatever problems you encounter, even those that are seemingly insurmountable, they will "come to pass."

The final board game is the **Game of Life**. A happy and meaningful life begins with a personal relationship with Jesus Christ (John 10:9–10).

Charles Trumbull said, "There is only one life that wins, and that is the life of Jesus Christ."[18] With Jesus as Lord and Savior, you are on the winning team in the game of life.

Prop: Each of the board games used in the talk.

48
It's What's on the Inside That Counts

A doctor cannot always tell what's wrong with you simply by looking at you. You may look healthy on the outside and still be very sick on the inside. X-ray's (pictures of the inside of a person) allow the doctor to look on the inside for things that may be wrong. No doctor can tell what is on the inside of a person by looking on his or her outside.

Samuel was to identify the one whom God had chosen to be the next king of Israel.

"When they came, he looked on Eliab and thought, 'Surely the LORD's anointed is before him.'

"But the LORD said to Samuel, 'Do not look on his appearance or on the height of his stature, because I have rejected him. For the LORD sees not as man sees: man looks on the outward appearance, but the LORD looks on the heart.'"—1 Samuel 16:6–7.

Like Samuel, people often look at a person from the outside, but God looks at a person's inside.

It's easy to make mistakes about people, as Samuel did, by looking only on the outside. A person may be beautiful outwardly but ugly inwardly, or not so beautiful outwardly and an absolute charming prince or princess inwardly. A person may appear outwardly to be a winner, when inwardly he is a loser; or outwardly a loser, when inwardly he is a winner.

A geode rock is ugly outwardly, but if cut open, its beautiful crystallized interior is revealed. The geode rock teaches us never to judge a book by its cover (judge a person by his or her outward appearance).

Some children have disabilities. Outwardly they don't look, walk, or talk like other children because of a sickness or injury. Don't make Samuel's mistake of judging their value or potential based upon the outside. Look at a person from the inside out as God does. It's not only the fair way to do it, but it is the only way for a person really to be known.

Seven of Jesse's son's filed by Samuel, but none were God's choice to be king. Finally, the youngest and least-expected to be God's choice (David) appeared before Samuel and was anointed to be the next king. Looking at people from the outside like Samuel did leads to big mistakes.

Don't judge others or yourself based upon outward appearance. God doesn't, so you shouldn't. God's acceptance of you and His unfailing love for you and others is not in any way based upon outward appearance (attraction, disabilities, abilities), but upon what's on the inside (the heart). Remember that's it's what's on the inside, not the outside appearance, that counts most.

Prop: An x-ray and a cut geode—a rock that's been cut open to reveal a beautiful crystallized interior.

49
David and Goliath the Bully

Never be a bully (a person who picks on someone with less strength than he has). A bully picks on a person who is shy, different, or lacking in the confidence or in the ability to defend himself. In an effort to belittle another, bullies use name-calling and teasing, separation from friends, bad-mouthing, and even fighting.

One of the oldest stories on bullying is that of David and Goliath. Daily, Goliath made fun of the Israelites in saying, "I defy the armies of Israel this day; give me a man, that we may fight together" (1 Samuel 17:10). The winner of that duel would determine whether the Philistines or the Israelites would be declared the victor of the day.

However, no soldier or person wanted to fight Goliath, who stood over nine feet tall and wore heavy battle armor—that is, not until a young man named David arrived willing to do what even the experienced soldiers in Saul's army were afraid to do.

David, with a sling and five stones, confronted Goliath. "Goliath walked out toward David with his shield bearer ahead of him, sneering in contempt at this ruddy-faced boy. 'Am I a dog,' he roared at David, 'that you come at me with a stick?' And he cursed David by the names of his gods. 'Come over here, and I'll give your flesh to the birds and wild animals!' Goliath yelled" (I Samuel 17:41–44 NLT).

Have you been threatened like David? Is there a bully at your school or neighborhood? Do you have a giant (bully) in

155

your life? Like David, you can trust God to help you overcome him or her.

If you are bullied, remember that all the bully says is an untruth, and share what happened with a school teacher and your parents. Don't be afraid to tell about being bullied, no matter what the threats may be.

If you see someone being bullied, speak up and ask the bully to stop and/or immediately go for help. It's important that you help the person being bullied in one or both of these ways.

In telling an adult about the bullying, you also are helping the bully. Bullies need to understand that there are rules they are expected to obey. They cannot always have their own way, go first in a game, win first place, get what they want, or control others. Adults can help them understand the rules so the bullying will end.

Prop: Reenact the story of David and Goliath to introduce the talk.

50
Live for God's Approval

Don't live life under the umbrella of another's approval. Do you take cues regarding the clothing you wear, the way you talk, your hairstyle, and the things you do from the expectations of others in an effort to please them?

If so, it is long past time to switch approval sources. You see, the ultimate source of approval is God; it's what He thinks of you that counts most. The foundational question then is not how others approve of your life, but how God does.

A young violinist, in ending his first concert, was applauded by a standing audience. Amid the approval of the crowd, his eyes stayed fixed the entire time upon an elderly man in the balcony.

The young violinist showed no emotion of joy until that man stood and applauded. You see, that elderly man was the young violinist's instructor, and he was concerned only with pleasing him.

Such was the attitude of the Apostle Paul with regard to Christ, for he testifies, "Obviously, I'm not trying to win the approval of people, but of God. If pleasing people were my goal, I would not be Christ's servant" (Galatians 1:10 NLT).

Live your life before an audience of ONE. If you please God with your life, it matters not if others accept you or not. All that matters in life and then in death is to hear our Lord say, "Well done, thou good and faithful servant"; or, in modern terms, "That a boy; that a girl!"

Prop: A violin.

51
Thanksgiving
Luke 17:11–19

Ten lepers cried out to Jesus for healing and were told to appear before the priests. "As they went" each was cleansed (verse 14). In gratitude, one of the ten who was healed fell prostrate at the feet of Jesus, giving thanks. A most searching question was then asked by Jesus: 'Were there not ten cleansed? Then where are the other nine?' (verse 17). Sadly, the other nine that Jesus had healed were nowhere to be found.

No other story in the Bible so clearly illustrates man's ingratitude. Do you liken yourself to the man who said thanks or to the other nine who didn't? God was pleased with the thankful man, not the unthankful men.

We have so much for which to be thankful: Jesus, the Bible, church, health, clothes to wear, food to eat, a home, friends, opportunity to attend school, and family. Let's not fail to thank God for His many blessings, and others for their acts of kindness toward us.

There are six things about expressing gratitude (giving thanks) that you should remember.

Thank You can never be overplayed. A person can never express gratitude too often.

Work hard at always saying, "Thank You." Cultivate the habit. "No duty is more urgent than that of returning thanks."[19]

Never assume another knows of your gratitude. Express it! The giver of a gift or kindness deserves an expression of gratitude and will be blessed by it. The purpose of giving the gift or doing the deed isn't to receive gratitude, but the person will be lifted when it is received.

Keep thank-you notes handy as a ready reminder to express thankfulness. It's what you write on the note that is important, not the design.

Don't delay in expressing thanks. Tomorrow may be too late.

First on the list of those to whom we should give thanks is God.

> For each new morning with its light,
> For rest and shelter of the night,
> For health and food, for love and friends,
> For everything Thy goodness sends."[20]
> —Ralph Waldo Emerson

To whom else do you need to say, "Thank You?" Today express gratitude to that person or those persons by a card, a letter, an e-mail, a phone call, or a gift.

Prop: A thank-you card, sufficient thank-you cards to distribute to all who are present, and a cross. In conclusion, you may say, "I will give you a thank-you note to use to express to God your gratitude for salvation and His many other blessings. Once the card is finished, place it at the foot of the cross here at the front of the church."

52
The Easter Message through Scripture Eggs
Matthew 28:6

Look at some colored plastic eggs that tell the story of Jesus' last week on earth.[21]

Let's see what's inside the **Blue Egg.** It's a donkey.

Did you know that Jesus rode a donkey into Jerusalem on the first day of the last week of His time on earth? Why did He ride a donkey and not a stallion? After all, He was the King of Kings.

At that period in history, kings rode donkeys in times of peace. Jesus was making a statement in riding the donkey. He had come into the world to die upon a Cross to bring peace to the heart of every person. And Jesus does bring peace to all who put their faith in Him as Lord and Savior.

What's inside the **Light Purple Egg?** It contains a cup and a piece of bread, which remind us of Jesus' Last Supper with the disciples on Thursday night.

The bread and cup spoke of Jesus' crucifixion, which was necessary for man's salvation and was to occur the next day. Believers observe the Lord's Supper to remember the price Jesus paid to make possible their salvation (rightness) to God (Matthew 26:27–28).

Here's an **Orange Egg.** What's inside of it? Praying hands.

Following the supper with the disciples, Jesus went into the Garden of Gethsemane to pray. He was deeply troubled, knowing that death was approaching the next day, and He asked God to give Him strength to face it. In times when you are facing things in life that trouble you, do as Jesus did and ask God for help.

What other eggs do we have in our Easter Basket? A **Light Pink Egg.** Inside it are some coins which tell how Judas sold Jesus out for thirty pieces of silver on Friday morning.

Judas pretended to be Jesus' friend, but then he betrayed Him with a kiss. Don't be a Judas, a pretender; be a real follower of Jesus. Never sell Jesus out for popularity, pleasure, or possession.

What's inside this **Green Egg?** A whip.

Upon being arrested following Judas' kiss, Jesus was put on trial by Pilate, who sentenced Him to die. Prior to His execution, Jesus was beaten with a leather whip made of rocks and metal. The lashing Jesus received left thirty-nine deep gashes on His precious back.

Hundreds of years earlier, the prophet Isaiah foretold that this would happen (Isaiah 53:5). All the torture Jesus endured before the cross, besides what He suffered upon the cross, speaks of His awesome love for you.

The **Light Yellow Egg** contains a crown which is symbolic of the crown of jagged thorns the soldiers pressed upon Jesus' head prior to compelling Him to carry the cross to Calvary.

Jesus deserved a royal crown, complete with precious jewels; instead, He got one that was extremely painful. Not everyone will love Jesus. Some will hate Him, as these soldiers did.

What's the next egg? It's a **Yellow Egg** which contains a cross.

Following the beating, Jesus carried a heavy cross three-fourths of a mile to Calvary. There His hands and feet were nailed to the cross. We look at Jesus on the Cross and ask why? Jesus died to make possible the forgiveness of sin, man's rightness with God.

Inside the **Light Green Egg** are dice. This part of the story is so heartbreaking.

As Jesus hung dying on the cross, soldiers gambled for His garment at its foot (Psalm 22:18). Jesus showed compassion toward them and the men who nailed Him to the cross by saying, "Father, forgive them; for they know not what they do" (Luke 23:34). Jesus is our example in showing love and forgiveness to those who bring us injury.

The **Purple Egg** contains a spear.

Soldiers would break the legs of criminals on the cross to speed up their death—they broke the legs of the two thieves next to Jesus but did not break Jesus' legs, for He was already dead. Simply to cover their backs by making sure Jesus was dead, the soldiers thrust a spear into His side (John 19:32–34).

What's another egg that remains in our basket? A **Cream Egg** which contains a tomb.

Joseph and Nicodemus requested permission to bury the body of Jesus, a request that was granted. These men had secretly believed in Jesus but at His death made it public. At the tomb, Jesus' body was wrapped in a burial cloth. Joseph and Nicodemus stood tall and firm for Jesus at His death but should have earlier. Always stand up for Jesus, whatever the costs or consequences may be.

Inside the **Pink Egg** is a stone.

Once Jesus' body was laid to rest in Joseph's tomb, a large stone that weighed one and one-half to two tons was rolled into its entrance to seal it. This was done to insure that the disciples would not steal the body of Jesus and later claim that He was raised from the dead. Roman soldiers guarded the tomb under the sentence of death should the body of Jesus be taken.

The final egg in our basket is the **Light Blue Egg.** The egg is empty.

Despite the stone and the guards, on Easter Sunday morning, just before sunrise, the stone was supernaturally rolled away, and Jesus was raised from the dead. Hear Matthew tell what happened. "And, behold, there was a great earthquake: for the angel of the Lord descended from heaven, and came and rolled back the stone from the door, and sat upon it" (Matthew 28:2). Later the angel said to the women who had come looking for Jesus, "He is not here: for he is risen, as he said. Come, see the place where the Lord lay" (verse 6).

Like the tomb, our hearts are empty and lifeless without Jesus. But Jesus specializes in coming into empty hearts and filling them with peace, love, and joy.

Prop: Purchase "Resurrection Eggs" at Family Christian Bookstore. Use an Easter basket in which to place the eggs, or utilize the egg carton in which they come. The talk may be presented in one or several services leading up to Easter.

53
A Special Birth Certificate
Matthew 1:23

My birth certificate tells when and where I was born, as well as many other things. It would be awesome to have the birth certificate of Jesus to study. Birth certificates like ours did not exist when Jesus was born, but if they had and a copy of His were available, it would be most informative. Based upon my own birth certificate and what the Bible states about Jesus' birth, what might a birth certificate for Jesus look like?

A birth certificate states the **child's name.** On my birth certificate, under the heading "Child's Name," the name Frank Ray Shivers is written. This is the name my parents gave me at birth.

Matthew 1:25 states, "And [Joseph] knew her not till she had brought forth her firstborn son: and he called his name JESUS." Jesus would be the name on His birth certificate, for it is the name God gave Him. It means "Savior." What a good name! Jesus came into the world to be our Savior and Lord.

It states the **place of birth.** My birth certificate states that I was born at Turberville Hospital, Escambia County, Florida.

Who can tell me where Jesus was born? Matthew 2:1 tells us. "Now when Jesus was born in Bethlehem of Judaea in the days of Herod the king." Jesus was born in Bethlehem in the land of Israel.

I was born in a hospital. Was Jesus? Luke 2:7 states, "And she brought forth her firstborn son, and wrapped him in swaddling clothes, and laid him in a manger; because there was no room for them in the inn." Jesus was born in a manger in a stable where cows or horses stayed.

It states the **date of birth**. My birth certificate states that I was born on August 21, 1949.

What date should be written on this birth certificate for the date of Jesus' birth? Though we are not certain in which year Jesus was born, December 25, 4 B.C. is a good date to insert. Did you know that when you write a date, you celebrate Jesus' birthday, for our calendar begins with the year He was born?

It states the name of the **father of the child.** My certificate reveals that Clark L. Shivers is my father. It states that he was thirty years old at the time of my birth and was a butcher.

Who was the father of Jesus? Luke tells us.

"And the angel said unto her, Fear not, Mary: for thou hast found favour with God.

"And, behold, thou shalt conceive in thy womb, and bring forth a son, and shalt call his name JESUS.

"He shall be great, and shall be called the Son of the Highest: and the Lord God shall give unto him the throne of his father David:

"And he shall reign over the house of Jacob for ever; and of his kingdom there shall be no end.

"Then said Mary unto the angel, How shall this be, seeing I know not a man?

"And the angel answered and said unto her, The Holy Ghost shall come upon thee, and the power of the Highest shall overshadow thee: therefore also that holy thing which shall be born of thee shall be called the Son of God."—Luke 1:30–35.

A Special Birth Certificate

Joseph was not the father of Jesus; he was only His guardian. His Father's name is the Lord God Almighty.

How old was God when Jesus was born? God is ageless. He is the same yesterday, today, and forever (Hebrews 13:8). Under "Occupation of Father," let's write Creator and Sustainer of the World. We could write much more, for God IS so much.

It states the name of the **mother of the child.** My certificate states that Mary Lois Shivers is my mother. It states she was twenty-one years old at my birth.

Luke tells us that the mother of Jesus was Mary (Luke 1:30). God would speak the Child into her womb, making His birth unique from any other. Mary was like you and I are. Jesus, not Mary, should be worshipped and followed.

It states who the **attendant at birth** was. Line 18b on my birth certificate states who the attendant was at my birth. It had three options one could check: "MD, Midwife or Other." MD (medical doctor) is checked on my certificate.

What block should be checked on Jesus' birth certificate? I think it would have to be the block labeled "Other." Who attended Jesus birth? Scripture tells us shepherds and wise men did. "The shepherds said one to another, Let us now go even unto Bethlehem, and see this thing which is come to pass, which the Lord hath made known unto us. And they came with haste, and found Mary, and Joseph, and the babe lying in a manger. And when they had seen it, they made known abroad the saying which was told them concerning this child" (Luke 2:15–17).

It asks **"How many other children are now living?"** My certificate indicates that at the time of my birth, I had only a brother.

God has only one Son, and this Son is sinless, the Savior of the world. But He has many other children. Every person who invites Jesus into his life as Lord and Savior becomes a child of God. Matthew tells us "For whosoever shall do the will of my Father which is in heaven, the same is my brother, and sister, and mother" (Matthew 12:50).

There is no room to write down on His certificate the names of all His spiritual brothers and sisters. His family consists of those who are saved. You can be included in His family if you desire.

It asks for **certification of birth.** My certificate reads, "I hereby certify that on the date stated above, this child was BORN ALIVE." I know I was born, because I have a birth certificate to prove it. A birth certificate proves the reality of life.

A birth certificate for Jesus would be a cool thing to have, but it would reveal only what is already known—that Jesus is a real Person. He was born alive and lives forevermore.

"He lives; He lives. Christ Jesus lives today. He walks with me and talks with me along life's narrow way....You ask me how I know He lives. He lives within my heart."

The only birth certificate available for Jesus is in the Bible, but hopefully this one I just shared helps you understand more about His birth and why He is so special.

Prop: A large posterboard formatted as a birth certificate that can be filled in as you share the talk and your personal birth certificate.

54
A Christmas Card from God
John 3:16

It's a joy to send out Christmas cards, and it's also wonderful to receive them. Think of special people to whom you may send a Christmas card.

Wouldn't it be awesome to get a Christmas card from God? It would be opened immediately and treasured forever.

This may come as a surprise to you, but in this big envelope marked "Special Delivery," God has sent you a Christmas card. Do you think I should open it now?

I wonder what message God wrote on this card for us. Do you think He wrote in it, "Santa Claus is coming to town," or, "Merry Christmas," or, "Happy Holidays"? I guess that will never be known unless I open it.

Here goes; I'm opening it. It's a Bible! Listen to God's message on its inside.

'I love you so much that I have given Jesus, my one and only Son, so that whoever believes in Him shall not perish, but have everlasting life.' That's a message straight from God's heart to everyone. God wants you to remember the real meaning of Christmas.

As you send and receive Christmas cards let them be reminders of God's Christmas card and the wonderful gift of Jesus that He gave to the world on that first Christmas.

Prop: A few Christmas cards and a Bible enclosed in a huge Christmas card stuffed in a special delivery package (UPS or FedEx box). Share the personal Christmas cards at the first of the talk.

55
Making Ready for Christmas
Luke 2:8–20

What are things people do to prepare for Christmas? The best way to get ready for Christmas is by doing what the shepherds did that first Christmas.

To get ready for Christmas, **you must know what the shepherds knew.** The shepherds knew that the Baby born in the manger of Bethlehem was no ordinary baby, but that He was the Messiah. Messiah means "Savior," so they knew that Jesus was the Savior of the world and opened their hearts to Him.

To get ready for Christmas, you must know what they knew—that the real meaning of Christmas is not decorated trees, presents, and mistletoe, but the celebration of the birth of Jesus Christ, the Savior of the world.

To get ready for Christmas, **you must show what the shepherds showed.** The shepherds were changed by Christ and showed this change to others. Let your parents, classmates, friends, and teachers see the difference Jesus has made in your life.

To get ready for Christmas, **you must go as the shepherds went.** The shepherds didn't keep the message of Christmas as a secret but went everywhere telling the story as they returned to their fields. Do the same, for everyone needs to hear the true meaning of Christmas.

Prop: A broom and dustpan. Begin the talk by sweeping around the stage or altar. Tell the children that you are making things ready for the Bible study time with them. Use this as a bridge into the talk, stating, "Christmas will soon be here, and we need to get ready, just as the shepherds did on that first Christmas."

56

What to Give Jesus This Christmas
Matthew 2:11

All of us are thinking about what gift to give family and friends at Christmas. It's not always easy picking out just the right present for everyone on our list, is it?

However, there is no problem in knowing just the right gift to give Jesus; it is the same as that which the Magi gave Him on that first Christmas. What gifts did the Wise Men give Jesus?[22]

The gift of Gold. The gift of gold would help Mary and Joseph provide the needs for the baby Jesus. As the Magi did, give Jesus the gift of your wealth (money) this Christmas. Regardless of its amount, He will be pleased and honored by your gift. In giving money to missions, world hunger, or church, you are giving a valuable gift to Jesus.

The gift of Frankincense. Frankincense (like the scented candles mom lights at home) was always used in sacrifices and worship to God. In giving this gift to Jesus, the Wise Men were worshiping Him. Everyone can give Jesus the gift of worship. Worship is adoring, praising, and loving Jesus.

The gift of Myrrh. The Magi also gave Jesus the gift of myrrh. Myrrh was used in ointments, salves, perfumes, and healing medicines. Mary of Bethany, in pouring myrrh over the head of Jesus, was serving Him. In giving myrrh to Jesus, the Wise Men were serving Him.

This Christmas, give Jesus the gift of work. Help an elderly person with yard work, or visit the nursing home, or assist your children's ministry leader in cleaning up after class.

What can you give Jesus this Christmas? Give Jesus the gift of your wealth, your worship, and your work. But above all, give Him the gift of your heart.

I read the story of a little boy who stood in an offering plate at church. In doing this, he was saying, "I offer to Jesus all I am." Will you do that?

Prop: A piece of gold jewelry, incense candle, and a tube of lotion wrapped separately in Christmas paper to symbolize the gifts of the Wise Men. Unwrap each as it is being discussed.

57
Decorating the Christmas Tree

From the beginning of the tradition of the Christmas tree, it was customary to decorate the tree with symbols of the newborn Christ.

The Tree. Have you ever wondered why people decorate a tree at Christmastime instead of decorating something else? Trees are decorated to symbolize how Jesus died upon a cross for the sin of the world. Jesus died upon a tree—on wood cut from a tree. Notice also that the limbs of the Christmas tree point upward toward Heaven as a reminder that Jesus came from Heaven to earth to save the world.

The Bulbs on the tree. A bulb is a symbol of a world globe, a reminder that Jesus came to save the whole world. "For God so loved the world…" (John 3:16).

The Lights on the tree. Jesus is God's Light shining in darkness and showing man how to live and be saved. Jesus said, "I am the light of the world" (John 8:12). A light makes the way plain when we are walking in darkness.

The Star. The Star on top of the tree speaks of how God guided the Wise Men to the manger and how He directs everyone who is seeking Jesus, helping them to find Him.

The Angels. The angel on the Christmas tree is a reminder of how the angelic chorus welcomed the birth of Jesus. "Hark, the herald angels sing, 'Glory to the newborn King!'"

The Cross. The cross hung on the tree is a reminder of the reason for Jesus' birth. He was born in the shadow of the cross, born to die to save men from their sins.

The Candy Cane. The candy cane upon the tree is a reminder of the shepherds' crooks—the crooks of the shepherds in the field that first Christmas night who, when they heard the angelic chorus, went to worship at the crib of the Christ child.

The Gifts. The presents underneath the tree remind us of God's great gift to the world—His only Son, Jesus Christ. This great gift was "wrapped in love." Have you received this wonderful gift?

Prop: A Christmas tree and decorations as described in the talk. Place each decoration onto the tree as it is discussed.

58
Christmas: The Word Tells the Story
Luke 2:12

The letters from the word *Christmas* tell the meaning of Christmas.

C is for the cradle in which the baby Jesus was born in Bethlehem's stable. He was not born in a palace or Holiday Inn, but in a stench-ridden barn.

H is for the heart of God that was manifested (seen) the day Christ was born. God loves us so much that He gave the first Christmas gift to us—His only Son.

"For God so loved the world, that he gave his only begotten Son, that whosoever believeth in him should not perish, but have everlasting life" (John 3:16).

"Oh, how He loves you! Oh, how He loves me! Oh, how He loves you and me!"

—Kurt Kaiser

R is for the reason Jesus came into this world. Jesus was born that first Christmas so He could die on a cross to save us from our sin. All of us have done wrong (sin), and that wrong (sin) separates us from God (Romans 3:23; 6:23). Jesus came to forgive that wrong so we would no longer be separated from God (Romans 5:8–9).

I is for the prophet Isaiah, who 750 years before Jesus' birth declared, "Therefore the Lord himself shall give you a sign; Behold, a virgin shall conceive, and bear a son, and shall call his name Immanuel" (Isaiah 7:14); "For unto us a child is born, unto us a son is given: and the government shall be upon his shoulder: and his name shall be called Wonderful,

Counsellor, The mighty God, The everlasting Father, The Prince of Peace. Of the increase of his government and peace there shall be no end" (Isaiah (9:6–7).

The New Testament lists fifty-two prophecies fulfilled in Jesus' birth and death, as stated in eighty-one passages in the Old Testament. If you need proof of the claims of Jesus, here it is! He had no control over the fulfillment of prophecies regarding His birth or death. It was clearly a God thing.

S   is for shepherds who were the first to hear the news of the Savior's birth.

"And there were in the same country shepherds abiding in the field, keeping watch over their flock by night.

"And, lo, the angel of the Lord came upon them, and the glory of the Lord shone round about them: and they were sore afraid.

"And the angel said unto them, Fear not: for, behold, I bring you good tidings of great joy, which shall be to all people.

"For unto you is born this day in the city of David a Saviour, which is Christ the Lord"—Luke 2:8–11.

Isn't it awesome that the first to hear of Jesus' birth were the poor and lowly shepherds? This speaks loudly to the world that God is no respecter of persons. Salvation belongs to all people.

T   is for the "tidings of great joy" which the angel announced (Luke 2:10). What was this Good News? The angel states that this Baby was the Savior of the world, which is expressed also in the meaning of His name, Jesus.

In essence, this Good News announcement was that salvation was now come to all men through the Lord Jesus Christ, who was born in the manger.

Christmas: The Word Tells the Story

M   is for the Magi who traveled from the east bearing gifts for the baby Jesus. Wise men still seek Jesus, and when they find Him, they give their lives to Him.

A   is for the adoration the baby Jesus received from the shepherds, the Magi, and the angels.

"And suddenly there was with the angel a multitude of the heavenly host praising God, and saying, Glory to God in the highest, and on earth peace, good will toward men" (Luke 2:13–14).

"Oh, come let us adore Him; Oh, come let us adore Him; Oh, come let us adore Him, Christ the Lord."

S   is for the sharing of the Good News of that first Christmas by the shepherds upon their departure from the stable.

"And they came with haste, and found Mary, and Joseph, and the babe lying in a manger. And when they had seen it, they made known abroad the saying which was told them concerning this child. And all they that heard it wondered at those things which were told them by the shepherds" (Luke 2:16–18).

Now it is our turn to go and tell the story of Christmas—that Jesus Christ came into this world to save sinners.

"Go tell it on the mountains, over the hills and everywhere. Go tell it on the mountains that Jesus Christ is born."

"We have heard the joyful sound—Jesus saves; Jesus saves! Spread the tidings all around—Jesus saves; Jesus saves! Tell to sinners far and wide—Jesus saves; Jesus saves!"

May you and I do just this!

Prop: Have a cutout of the letters in the word *Christmas,* and as each point is taught, have a staff member or child hold a letter. They continue holding the letter until the word is spelled.

59
The Talking Cross
Matthew 27:31

Perhaps you have decorated the Christmas tree with your parents. Now let's decorate the cross.

The cradle in Bethlehem is inseparable from the Cross at Calvary. To understand the meaning of the cradle of Jesus, you need to understand the message of His cross.

What decorations (objects) ought to go on the cross to tell the story of Jesus' death?

A **Coin** to speak of Judas' betrayal of Jesus (Matthew 26:15). Judas sold Jesus out for thirty pieces of silver. Will you sell Him out for popularity, fun, toys, or friends? Don't sell Jesus out like Judas did.

A **Sword** to speak of Peter's rash act in severing Malchus' ear (Matthew 26:51). Jesus' rebuke of Peter for what he did teaches us that Christians are to love all people, even those who seek their harm.

A **Rooster** to speak of Peter's denial of Jesus three times before the 'cock crowed' (Matthew 26:74). Peter cowered down when he should have championed up for Jesus.

Are you afraid to speak up for Jesus when others don't think it's cool? Never be ashamed of Jesus.

A **Crown** of jagged thorns to tell how the soldiers made fun of Jesus' claim to be the King of Kings (John 19:2). The crown was a wreath similar to that which athletes would compete to gain, except it was made of pointed thorns and briers. One can only imagine the pain that Jesus experienced when the crown of thorns was pressed firmly upon His head.

A **Purple Robe** to speak of how the Roman soldiers made fun of Jesus (John 19:2).

A **Whip** to tell of Jesus' beating (John 19:1). In the movie *The Passion of the Christ,* a scene shows Jesus being whipped with the Roman cat-o'-nine-tails. The pain Jesus suffered in this beating reveals His awesome love for us.

Two Gloves (for two hands) to tell how Pilate washed his hands of the matter (Matthew 27:24). Pilate attempted to remain neutral concerning Jesus by washing his hands of what to do with Him, but He couldn't.

No man can be indecisive about Jesus. He must decide to follow Him or not follow Him.

A **Hammer and Spikes** to tell how Jesus was nailed to the cross (John 20:25).

An **INRI Sign** like the one which Pilate had attached to the cross. This meant "This is Jesus of Nazareth, the King of the Jews" (Matthew 27:37; Mark 15:26; Luke 23:38; John 19:19). Pilate was asked to change the sign to read, "He said He is the King of the Jews." Pilate refused to do so, saying, "What I have written I have written" (John 19:22). All soon came to realize that what he had written was the truth.

Dice to tell how the soldiers at the foot of the cross gambled for Jesus' garment (John 19:23–24). Jesus hung dying, and Roman soldiers played games at the foot of His cross.

People still play games, giving no attention to the fact and meaning of the death of Jesus Christ. Many in the church are playing games about being a Christian.

A **Sponge** filled with vinegar like they gave Jesus to prolong His pain and torment (John 19:29). Offering Jesus something to drink was no kind gesture. The purpose of the hyssop with the sponge full of vinegar was to prolong His suffering.

A **Spear** to tell of the piercing of Jesus' side to insure His death (John 19:34). Routinely, the legs of those being crucified were broken to insure death would come more quickly, but this was not necessary in the case of Jesus, for He was already dead when the soldiers checked on Him. To assure that He was dead, they simply pierced His side with a sword.

The **Ten Commandments** to tell why Jesus had to die. Man's failure to keep God's Law (the Ten Commandments) separated him from God. Nothing short of Jesus' death upon a cross could make possible man's forgiveness and rightness with God.

A **Ladder** to indicate how they got Jesus' body down from the cross. Soldiers used a ladder to remove Jesus' body from the cross. Joseph and Nicodemus received permission to bury the body of Jesus in a tomb nearby (Matthew 27:57–60).

A **Heart** to tell of God's great love for the world in giving His only Son to make possible man's salvation (John 3:16). The love of God for the whole world is demonstrated at the cross.

"Oh, how He loves you! Oh, how He loves me! Oh, how He loves you and me!"

—Kurt Kaiser

A **Door** to tell how Jesus, in His death and resurrection, became man's way to reconciliation (rightness) with God (John 10:9). The Door (Jesus) to forgiveness of sin and a right

183

relationship with God stands wide open for all to enter (John 6:37).

Prop: A large cross and each of the crucifixion symbols cited in the talk. Attach each symbol to the Cross as you tell the children what it means.

60
Candy Bars and Christmas

Various kinds of candy tell the Christmas story.

It wasn't *Baby Ruth* in the manger that first Christmas, but Baby Jesus. "And she shall bring forth a son, and thou shalt call his name JESUS: for he shall save his people from their sins" (Matthew 1:21).

It wasn't on *Fifth Avenue* where Jesus was born, but in Bethlehem's manger. "Now when Jesus was born in Bethlehem of Judaea in the days of Herod the king" (Matthew 2:1).

It wasn't the *Three Musketeers,* but the three Wise Men who came to see Jesus. "Now when Jesus was born in Bethlehem of Judaea in the days of Herod the king, behold, there came wise men from the east to Jerusalem" (Matthew 2:1).

It wasn't the *Milky Way* the Wise Men saw, but a star. "Saying, Where is he that is born King of the Jews? for we have seen his star in the east, and are come to worship him" (Matthew 2:2).

It wasn't *Zero* that the Wise Men brought, but four gifts. "When they had heard the king, they departed; and, lo, the star, which they saw in the east, went before them, till it came and stood over where the young child was. When they saw the star, they rejoiced with exceeding great joy. And when they were come into the house, they saw the young child with Mary his mother, and fell down, and worshipped him: and when they had opened their treasures, they presented unto him gifts; gold, and frankincense, and myrrh" (Matthew 2:9–11).

It wasn't *Mr. Goodbar* who wanted to kill Jesus, but bad King Herod. "Then Herod, when he had privily called the wise men, enquired of them diligently what time the star appeared. And he sent them to Bethlehem, and said, Go and search diligently for the young child; and when ye have found him, bring me word again, that I may come and worship him also" (Matthew 2:7–8).

It wasn't *Nerds* who watched sheep in the fields the night of Jesus' birth, but shepherds. "And there were in the same country shepherds abiding in the field, keeping watch over their flock by night" (Luke 2:8).

It wasn't the *Raisinets* the shepherds heard singing, but the angels. "And, lo, the angel of the Lord came upon them, and the glory of the Lord shone round about them: and they were sore afraid. And the angel said unto them, Fear not: for, behold, I bring you good tidings of great joy, which shall be to all people. For unto you is born this day in the city of David a Saviour, which is Christ the Lord. And this shall be a sign unto you; Ye shall find the babe wrapped in swaddling clothes, lying in a manger. And suddenly there was with the angel a multitude of the heavenly host praising God, and saying, Glory to God in the highest, and on earth peace, good will toward men" (Luke 2:9–14).

It wasn't *Jolly Ranchers* in Bethlehem's stable that holy night, but joyful saints.

It was *Good & Plenty* what God did that first Christmas in giving Jesus. "And she shall bring forth a son, and thou shalt call his name JESUS: for he shall save his people from their sins" (Matthew 1:21). It was *GOOD* in that He loved us enough to send His only Son, Jesus, into this world. It was *PLENTY* in what Jesus came into the world to do—to forgive sin, making man right with God.

Candy Bars and Christmas

Jesus is the Christmas Gift that keeps on giving throughout the year and throughout life.

Prop: Purchase the various candy bars that will be used in the talk and hold up each one as you discuss that particular point. Celebrate Christmas at the talk's end by throwing out the candy bars to the children.

61
The Unopened Invitation
Revelation 22:17

What just fell out of my Bible onto the floor? Oh, it's just a letter I got last month. It must be some type of invitation. I really must open it sometime. It does look interesting, but I will read it later. Now what was I going to talk about?

On second thought, I ought to open the invitation now. I think it's from Billy. He's the richest, coolest kid in town and has a ton of toys. It would be awesome for him to invite me over to his house. But he probably never will.

I've heard Billy has go-carts for friends to ride. Wouldn't it be just awesome to ride in one of them? I probably never will. I had better get back to my sermon for today. Let's see now—I need to read something from the Bible.

By the way, I heard Billy has his own candy store and he lets friends eat all they want. If fortunate enough to get an invitation to go to his house, I would take some Snickers, fudge, Milky Way bars and Reese's cups. What would you take? It would be really neat to get an invitation from Billy to visit his house.

(At this point, an adult should suggest you open the envelope immediately. This will get the kids crying out for you to do so.)

You know, this letter just may be the invitation I have desired. Do you think it is? Could it really be an invitation to a party or something?

(Study the envelope and say, "Yep, I think it may be an invitation.")

You know, someday I must really open this envelope! It might be an invitation. Do you think I should open it now with all these people around to see?

(Let the kids encourage you to open it, and then finally do so.)

Sure enough, it is the invitation I have waited on for such a long time—one to attend a party at Billy's house. Yes, I will go. Sure I will go. Is he kidding? Nothing can keep me from being there.

Now, when is the party? Let's see. It says, "You are invited to attend my party Thursday, Dec. 8." Oh no, that was yesterday! I waited too long to open the invitation. The party is over. I missed it. I should have opened the invitation sooner.

Did you know that God has sent you an invitation? He did, and it is in this Book. The invitation is for you to become a Christian. "Behold, I stand at the door, and knock: if any man hear my voice, and open the door, I will come in to him" (Revelation 3:20). The invitation is offered to every person in the world, which surely includes you.

Someday it will be too late to accept God's invitation. Just as I missed the party, you may miss your chance to go to Heaven. Open your heart now to Jesus, taking Him up on His invitation to be His child. Don't wait too long to open Jesus' invitation and respond to it.[23]

Prop: A sealed letter of invitation to a party tucked inside a Bible.

62
The Candy Cane Sermon

The candy cane tells the message of Christmas.[24]

Let's allow the white base of the candy to speak of the virgin birth and sinless life of Jesus and how He washes our sin away at salvation, making us white as snow.

Let's allow the candy's hardness tell us about how Jesus is the strong rock of refuge who provides His children protection and about His promises to be as firm as a rock.

The candy is sweet. Let's allow that to stand for the sweetness of God's Word. David said the Word of God was sweeter than honey to his taste (Psalm 119:103).

Let's imagine that the three small red stripes tell of Jesus' being beaten by the Roman soldiers with the Roman cat-o'-nine-tails and of the big red stripe of His blood shed on the cross that makes possible man's salvation.

Finally, look at the shape of the candy. It is formed in the letter *J.* Let that stand for the name of Jesus, who came that first Christmas to be the Savior of the world.

When you turn the cane upside down, the *J* becomes a staff or shepherd's crook, reminding us that Jesus is the Great Shepherd, ever guarding and providing care for His children.

Let the candy cane help you to share the message of Christmas with friends.

Prop: A gigantic candy cane. Small candy canes to give the children following the talk.

63
Socks for Christmas

What Christmas presents are you hoping to get? Maybe one gift will be socks. That's an exciting present, isn't it? I recall getting at least ten pairs of socks for Christmas. Certain kind of socks tells the Christmas story.

Wool Socks picture the shepherds to whom the angels appeared that first Christmas (Luke 2:8). The announcement of Jesus' birth was not made first to a King, but to the common man, mere shepherds who tended to sheep.

Angel Socks picture the angels who appeared to the shepherds telling the news of Jesus' birth in the manger at Bethlehem (Luke 2:9).

Hiking Socks picture the Wise Men, who traveled from the East following the heavenly "star" to the manger in Bethlehem so they could present gifts and worship the Christ child (Matthew 2:1–2; 9–11).

Smelly Socks picture the stinking stable which housed cattle or donkeys where Jesus was born (Luke 2:16). Jesus was not born in a Holiday Inn, but in a stench-ridden stable.

Baby Socks picture the baby Jesus born on that first Christmas (Luke 2:16). Jesus was born in the shadow of the cross. He came to provide salvation for all the people of the world.

Running Socks picture Joseph, Mary, and the baby Jesus fleeing to Egypt to prevent King Herod from finding and killing Jesus (Matthew 2:13). The socks also picture the shepherds who ran to tell everybody what they had heard and seen regarding the Christ child (Luke 2:20).

When someone is talking too much, another may say, "Put a sock in your mouth" (be quiet). Don't put a sock in your mouth when it comes to sharing Jesus with others.

Real Religion Socks picture the birth, death, and resurrection of Jesus to save the world from sin as the real, true deal. Jesus is the only hope of salvation. Everything and everyone else that offers it is false. In receiving socks at Christmas, do not grumble; rather, happily use them to tell others the story of Christmas.[25]

Prop: The seven types of socks shared in the sermon.

64
Christmas Bulbs Light Up Christmas

Four large Christmas bulbs tell the message of Christmas.

The **Black Bulb** tells why Jesus came that first Christmas. Man disobeyed God (sinned), resulting in separation from God (Romans 3:23). Jesus came into the world to enable man to become right with God.

The **Red Bulb** tells what Jesus did to make man right with God. He died upon a cross, making it possible for man's sin to be forgiven and enabling man to become right with God. (Romans 5:8)

The **White Bulb** tells what happens upon salvation. At the moment of conversion (receiving Jesus as Savior), Jesus washes the black sin in the heart away, making the person white as snow (I John 1:7).

The **Gold Bulb** tells of Heaven, the believer's eternal home. Jesus came into the world not only to save us from Hell, but also to take us to live with Him forever in His Home.[26]

Prop: Four superlarge Bulbs of the colors stated.

65
Objects That Tell of Christmas
Luke 19:10

Which of the following objects remind you of Christmas—stockings, Frosty the Snowman, fire truck, reindeer, snow sleigh, rescue ring, ambulance, helicopter? Stockings hung on the chimney with care, reindeer, and sleighs all remind us of Christmas and are a fun part of this glad holiday. But the other objects have more to do with Christmas than these items commonly associated with the day, for Christmas is about being rescued.

In the first Christmas message, the angel told the shepherds, 'Do not be afraid, for I bring you good news…This night in Bethlehem is born to you a Savior, which is Jesus Christ the Lord' (Luke 2:10). The angel was announcing the news that God had sent a Rescuer into the world to save man from sin.

You and I need this Rescuer (Jesus) because we have sinned, disobeyed God (Romans 3:23; 6:23). Sin has separated man from God; but Jesus, the Rescuer, is able to forgive sin, making things right between God and man.

In the same manner that a rescue ring can save you when drowning, a fire truck can save you from a burning building and a helicopter can save you from a flood, Jesus can save you from the consequences of sin (wasted life on Earth and Hell hereafter).

Enjoy Christmas, and always remember that it's more about a Rescuer than Frosty the Snowman or Rudolph.[27]

Prop: A rescue ring, fire truck and helicopter.

66
Are You Ready for Christmas?
Isaiah 9:6

Are you ready for Christmas? What's happening at your home to prepare for Christmas?[28]

What is all that noise I hear? It's Jimmy cleaning the church. "Jimmy, why are you cleaning the church in the middle of my talk to these boys and girls?"

He replies, "I'm sorry about that, but this just can't wait. Christmas is almost here, and the church has to be ready for it."

"What do you mean 'ready for it'?"

"Christmas," Jimmy responds. "It has to be ready for Christmas. The church must be ready for Christmas by having the floors clean and pews dusted."

"Jimmy, that's not how we get ready for Christmas."

"If that's not it, then how do we get ready for Christmas?" Jimmy asks.

You don't get ready for Christmas by the outward stuff (point to the broom and dust cloth), but by the inward stuff (point to the heart) you do. The way to really get ready for Christmas is not by hanging the stockings, decorating the tree, buying presents, and checking off the calendar day by day as I did at your age, but by making room in your heart for Jesus Christ.

Prop: A broom and dust cloth. Invite a leader or staff member of the church to act out Jimmy's role.

67

No Room for You
Luke 2:7; John 1:11

Joseph and Mary tried to find a room in Bethlehem's inn, but the innkeeper said, "I have no room for you."

Have you ever been told, "I don't have room for you?" If so, you know how badly hearing those words hurt. Perhaps Mom or Dad said, "I have no room for you," and then abandoned you. Maybe these words were heard from a coach when you wanted to be on the team: "I have no room for you." Perhaps when you asked for help from a teacher, he or she said, "I have no room for you." You wanted to attend a big party, and select others were invited, but you were not. They said, "I have no room for you." Maybe these words were heard at church, "We don't have room for you."

Jesus knows how deeply these few words hurt, for He heard them time and again throughout His life. While He was in the womb of Mary, He heard them from the innkeeper. When He was nailed to the cross, Jesus heard the world saying, "We don't have room for you."

Scripture tells us, "He [Jesus] came unto his own, and his own received him not" (John 1:11). Jesus still hears the same words as He seeks entrance into men's hearts. "We don't have room for you."

Jesus sympathizes with everyone who hears these words and gives assurance that no one will ever hear these painful words of rejection from Him. With open arms, Jesus says to you, "I have room for you and always will, no matter what happens."[29]

The big question is, do you have room for Jesus?

Prop: Scenes of Jesus' life that are shared in the talk (actual or on posterboard). "No room for Jesus" signs to attach to each scene as it is discussed. An "I have room for you" sign from Jesus to the boys and girls hung around a cross as the talk concludes.

68
Toolbox for the New Year
Philippians 2:12

The State newspaper had an article that stated, "You can't build a city without tools. What are the tools for development in Columbia and USC's toolboxes?"[30]

The news story caused me to think that a person can't build a life without tools either. Let's look into the New Year's Tool Box to see what tools are needed to build a happy life in the new year.

The Tool of Scripture. "And that from a child thou hast known the holy scriptures, which are able to make thee wise unto salvation through faith which is in Christ Jesus. All scripture is given by inspiration of God, and is profitable for doctrine, for reproof, for correction, for instruction in righteousness: That the man of God may be perfect, throughly furnished unto all good works" (2 Timothy 3:15–17).

God's Word equips the Christian for the walk and work of life. It is a mirror that shows sin and an instruction manual on how to live (Psalm 119:105). The Bible speaks to every issue of life that man confronts. Use it often.

The Tool of the Church. The church is a place of fellowship with Christians, instruction about Jesus, help in living for Jesus, and worship of Jesus. "But exhort one another daily, while it is called To day; lest any of you be hardened through the deceitfulness of sin" (Hebrews 3:13). The church is a place where we spur (encourage) each other in living for Jesus.

The Tool of Prayer. Prayer is talking to God from the heart. Prayer is praising God for who He is and what He has done. It is asking God for needs that others and you have. It is asking God to pardon (forgive) wrong. It is asking God to protect you and to give you power to resist temptation to do wrong.

When you pray, remember that God is concerned about what concerns you.

The Tool of Forgiveness. In the new year, when you have been hurt by another's words or actions, reach into this toolbox and pull out the tool of forgiveness. Forgiving others, though not always easy, is always right.

Jesus said, "'Be alert. If you see your friend going wrong, correct him. If he responds, forgive him. Even if it's personal against you and repeated seven times through the day, and seven times he says, "I'm sorry, I won't do it again," forgive him.'" (Luke 17:3–4 The Message)

The Tool of Soul Winning. God wants you to tell others of Christ (Acts 1:8). Never be ashamed to let others know you are a Christian, and never be a coward about sharing the message of Jesus.

Tools in a toolbox will not be of any value unless used. Use the tools in the toolbox of life regularly in the new year and it will be a "Happy New Year."

Prop: A large toolbox (letter it "Toolbox for the New Year") with objects that symbolize each of the tools in the talk. While you are speaking, take from the toolbox the tool under discussion and hold it before the children.

69
What's on the Table?
Romans 12:1–2

What was on your heart's table last year? Was it stuff that was spiritually healthy or unhealthy?

Whatever bad spiritual stuff was on it must be removed and replaced with that which will help you be more like Jesus in the new year. What spiritual dishes need to be set on your heart's table for the new year?

First, place on the table the **Platter of Communion with God.** This platter will be the largest dish on the table, because nothing is more important to the Christian than the study of God's Word and prayer.

Place on the table of life the **Finger Bowl of Cleansing by God.** In the new year, you will need to use this bowl often when you do wrong. The time to ask forgiveness of God is the moment following the wrong committed (1 John 1:9).

Place on the table of life the **Glass of the Fullness of God.** God wants to fill your life to overflowing with His love, peace, power, and joy. Keep drinking from Jesus, the Fountain of Living Water, that you may stay full (Ephesians 5:18).

Place on the table the **Plate of the Church.** Make room on your table for church attendance in the new year. Go to Church to grow in Christ's likeness and to help others to do the same.

No table would be complete without eating utensils, so you need the **Silverware of Service to God.** What will you do for Jesus in the new year? Though you cannot do the same work as an adult, there is much that you can do and that you should do.

The young boy gave his five loaves and two fishes for Jesus to use. Do the same by giving Him your five's and two's. You have two hands with five fingers each, two feet with five toes each, two eyes, two ears, and two lips. Tell Jesus that in the new year, He can use your five's and two's any way He desires.

Don't forget about the **Dessert Dish of Sweet Fellowship with Other Christians.** Most likely when you are thinking of ice cream socials, you think of fellowship time with other believers. Definitely put this dish on the table of your life for the new year, for every Christian needs other Christians for help and encouragement in living for Jesus.

The table is now set for a Happy New Year. Let's be sure to eat out of every dish on it throughout the year.

Prop: A table (labeled "Table for the New Year"), complete with tablecloth and table settings. While speaking, place on the table the dish that symbolizes the truth presented.

70
Take Aim at the Right Targets
1 Corinthians 9:26

Archery is a fun sport. With bow and arrow in hand, one takes aim at the target and then releases the arrow. A person's aim determines whether the target will be hit or missed.

In the new year, I challenge you to take aim at several important targets that will boost your spiritual growth (make you become more like Jesus).

In the new year, aim at "digging out" of salvation its fullest potential (benefit) through the discipline (practice) of prayer, Bible study, and church worship.

Be intentional about (take aim at) telling others about Jesus at school and in the neighborhood. We are most like Jesus when we are telling others the message of salvation.

In the new year, aim at being clean in mind and body. Say a loud no to Satan's temptations to sin. Use caution in viewing the Internet or television, for what one sees influences what one does. Refuse to allow friends to persuade you to do wrong.

Aim at staying focused on God's plan. Even though you are but a child, God often calls one of your age to be a pastor, a missionary, an evangelist, a teacher, or one who serves in another full-time ministry. Stay focused on this target, refusing to be sidetracked or shipwrecked, if you have been called into a particular ministry by God.

Aim at putting in place in your life spiritual protectors, things that will prevent you from drifting away from God.

Solomon tells of a lazy man who failed to fortify a wall (Proverbs 24:30–34). At the first, this man had a strong wall, but due to his laziness and neglect of discipline, the wall toppled to the ground.

Without protection, the wall of your life also will topple to the ground. Protect it by making sure nothing that would injure it is permitted into it.

Several great protectors of our heart's fortress are Christian friends, children's ministers, parents, prayer, Bible reading, and church worship. Aim at these targets in the new year.

Prop: A large archery target, bow and arrow; toy miniature arrows (or paper targets) to give to the children to remind them of the lesson.

Endnotes

[1] C. H. Spurgeon. *Come Ye Children.* www.spurgeon.org/misc/cyc14.htm.

[2] Ibid.

[3] Franklin Graham with Donna Lee Toney. *Billy Graham in Quotes.* (Nashville: Thomas Nelson, 2011), 42.

[4] Adapted from a talk by Russell Dean, heard by the author at Camp McCall, 1975.

[5] David Beatty. "It's Different Now." Namethathymn.com, accessed September 6, 2012.

[6] Adapted from an unknown source.

[7] Horatio Spafford, 1873. Music: Philip Bliss, 1876.

[8] Harriet E. Buell. "I'm a Child of the King." 1877

[9] The story's main headings are not original, but are taken from an unknown source.

[10] Adapted from a children's sermon heard at Camp McCall, Pickens, South Carolina, 1975.

[11] Adapted from www.firstpresby.org/past300.htm, First Presbyterian Church in Pitman, New Jersey.

[12] Adapted from a sermon by Oral Roberts which the writer heard on television, 1971.

[13] Variously attributed to S. E. L. and A. C. Palmer (1845–1882).

[14] Inspired by Hyles, Jack. *Salvation Is More Than Being Saved.* (Hammond, IN: Hyles-Anderson Publishers, 1985), chapter 18.

[15] Greg Laurie. https://www.harvest.org/devotional/archive/.../2012-03-19.html, accessed September 2, 2012.

[16] Walter Knight. *Knight's Illustrations for Today*, p. 158.

[17] Author Unknown

[18] http://www.bereanpublishers.com/the-life-that-wins, accessed September 25, 2012.

[19] Unknown.

[20] Ralph Waldo Emerson. "49 Gratitude Quotes and A Poem of Thanksgiving." daringtolivefully.com/gratitude-quotes, accessed September 2, 2012.

[21] Resurrection Eggs. Family Life (Family Christian Bookstore). Adapted.

[22] Adapted from Schofied, Joseph A. "Gold, Frankincense and Myrrh", *Stimulating Object Talks.* (Grand Rapids: Baker Book House, 1955), 133.

[23] Adapted from Bass, C. W. *Sparkling Object Sermons for Children.* (Grand Rapids: Baker Book House, 1982), 20–21.

[24] The author avoids citing what is shared as if it were historical fact. It is used simply as an illustration of the Christmas message. No documentation may be found regarding the authenticity of the claim that a candy maker in Indiana designed the cane to proclaim the message of Christmas.

[25] Based on Talks2Children.wordpress.com/2010/11/19/socks-for-christmas, accessed November 27, 2010.

[26] Adapted from www.creativeyouthideas.com/blog/evangelism_ideas/christmas_tree_evangelism, accessed February 12, 2013.

[27] luke-2v8-20-kids-talk-rescue-not-reindeers.pdf, accessed February 12, 2013.

[28] Hinchey, Donald. 5-Minute Message for Children. (Loveland, Colorado: Group Publications, 1992), 86–87.

[29] Adapted from Max Lucado. Maxlucado.com/general/no-room/, accessed February 8, 2013.

[30] *The State,* November 22, 2005.

www.ingramcontent.com/pod-product-compliance
Lightning Source LLC
Chambersburg PA
CBHW052038090426
42739CB00010B/1952